DATE DUE	
NOV 0 7 1 2006	
JUL 2 3 2007	
MAR 0 3 2008	

DEMCO, INC. 38-2931

ZAP!

ALSO BY SCOTT COHEN

Meet the Makers
Jocks

ZAP!
The Rise and Fall of ATARI

Scott Cohen

MCGRAW-HILL BOOK COMPANY

New York   St. Louis   San Francisco
Toronto   Hamburg   Mexico

123456789 FGR FGR 87654

ISBN 0-07-011543-5

Library of Congress Cataloging in Publication Data

Cohen, Scott.
    ZAP! the rise and fall of Atari.
    1. Atari, Inc.—History.   2. Electronic games
industry—United States—History.   I. Title.
HD9993.E454A853   1984   338.4'7794   83–22198
ISBN 0-07-011543-5
Book Design by Nancy Dale Muldoon

FOR GILBO

THE AUTHOR would like to thank Gordon Bishop, Susan Blond, Boom Boom, Ernie Brooks, Suzie Crocker, Jack Freeman, Gail Greene, Lisa Grotheer, Robert Hicks, Danny Himmelfarb, Gary Kenton, Huey Lewis, Susan Lee Merrow, Glenn O'Brien, Richard Pine, Michael Rosenberg, Kathleen Stein, Stephanie, and a number of people who provided inside information and would rather not be mentioned by name.

Special thanks to David Cohen.

"The total amount requested for aid to all of Central America in 1984 is about $600 million; that is less than one-tenth of what Americans will spend this year on coin-operated video games. . . ."

—*from the President's speech to Congress*

Author's Note

"THEY have seen our demise and named it Atari," declared Clive Davis, president of Arista Records, in a *Billboard* magazine editorial. He was responding to fearful comments by industry biggies that video games meant "the end of recorded music as we know it."

Davis admitted video games were hot. "Certainly we're competing for that lunch money, for those allowances, but to think these games will supplant music is absurd." He wound up by saying, "You can't hum a video game or dance to its beat."

Of course Clive Davis was wrong. People could dance to it, to the tune of billions of dollars a year. In 1981 alone, five billion dollars and seventy-five thousand man-years were spent at video machines and a billion dollars more were spent on home video game entertainment. That's twice the amount reported that year by all the casinos in Las Vegas combined. Video games raked in almost twice what Hollywood grossed; three times the combined TV revenues and gate receipts of major-league baseball, basketball and football; and four times the amount of money spent on records and rock concerts. People hummed along, tapped their toes, bobbed their heads and shook their hips to the video beat, but they couldn't snap their fingers to it—they were too busy pushing buttons.

I've seen the best minds—and feet—of my generation destroyed in arcades, bowling alleys, pizza parlors, candy stores, five-and-dimes, and 7-Elevens. I've watched lunchless teens throw away their allowances on Space Invaders; grown men in suits and ties tear their hair out and cry over Asteroids; Pac-maniacs crawl through the streets at dawn looking for a video fix. I've seen homes broken, marriages ruined, careers destroyed by video games. An 18-year-old was murdered in a bar on Long Island over a game of Pac-man. Another player in Illinois died of a heart attack while playing Berserk. I'd seen these vidiots waste their money and their lives, and I wanted to meet the inventors of these games. In 1982 I flew out to Silicon Valley (California), "the cradle of electronic civilization," to visit Atari, once the fastest-growing company in the history of the country. The following is a modern fable, as related by those who were there, about a company that went from $0 to $2 billion in ten years and then blew it in less than a year.

1

FROM THE AIR, Silicon Valley, with its gridlike streets, low, rectangular buildings, and identical rows of industrial parks, looks like a giant microchip. Buildings look like transistors, parking lots like resistors, and the on-and-off ramps of the freeway that connect the Valley with the outside world look like the lands around the edges of the microchip. Moffett Field blimp hangar, the largest landmark in the Valley, could easily be taken for an ROM, an array of memory cells that form the largest landmark on the chip, except you need a microscope to see it.

Silicon Valley begins in Palo Alto, at Bill Hewlett's garage, where in 1939 he and Dave Packard, a fellow Stanford alumnus, launched Hewlett-Packard, the highly regarded, multibillion-dollar granddaddy of electronics firms. From there it sprawls south for about twenty miles, to San Jose, taking in a dozen towns along the way. Every day another

1

chip manufacturer, supplier, or chip-related company pops up, making the Valley the world's semiconductor capital, just as Castroville, to the southwest, is the artichoke capital. Until the mid-1950s the fertile Santa Clara Valley, as it is formally called, was a veritable fruit bowl—acres upon acres of apricot, cherry, pear, and plum orchards; half the world's prunes came from here. Today, of the original hundred thousand acres of orchards, only thirteen hundred remain. It's as if an engineer in the mountains had pushed a button and the prunes had turned into microchips.

Whiz-kid engineers, hot programmers, maverick entrepreneurs, headhunters, venture capitalists, and industrial spies come to the Valley in droves. They know it's not unusual to land a job one day and start a new business the next, taking along company secrets, a few employee buddies, and maybe some equipment. They know technology is evolving so fast here that any self-starting, fast-moving, money-grubbing egomaniac with the right idea at the right time can wind up filthy rich. Most put in twelve-hour days, seven days a week, for months and end up depressed, divorced, and drunk, just like the prospectors of California's first Gold Rush.

*   *   *

Fog doesn't roll into the Valley the way it rolls into San Francisco. Smog from San Francisco and Oakland blows through on its way to San Jose. The air is dusty and yellow, especially in the summer, and the barren, parched foothills to the east look like big baked potatoes that rolled down from Idaho. Their size and prehistoric topography offer a striking contrast to the low, flat, regular patterns of industrial parks spread out like a checkered tablecloth below them. The streets look like they were stamped out by a huge waffle iron. The fruit trees, knocked down by bulldozers, have been replaced by prefabricated industrial plants—no pun intended.

Most buildings around here are called "tilt-ups." They're ideal for the start-up companies that occupy them. One day a helicopter flies in, puts up the walls and the roof, and the next day a company moves in, sometimes before the landscaper puts in the shrubbery. From the outside it's impossible to tell what's going on inside these buildings, one indistinguishable from another. The nameplates out front don't give a clue—Xicor, Qume, Zylog ... Driving around the Valley is like driving around Beverly Hills and coming upon the homes of the stars. There's Pickfair Manor, there's Cary Grant's mansion, here's where Pat Boone lives. There's National Semiconductor, there's Control Data, here's Intel. If it weren't for the nameplates, it would be hard to pick out Atari without putting your ear to the wall. Then you would hear that familiar thumping, bumping, and beeping coming from inside.

*　　*　　*

The busiest intersection in the Valley is at the corner of San Antonio and El Camino Real, in Mountain View. There are four shopping centers—four immense shopping centers—at this intersection. On the southeast corner is Avcar, a warehouse-size liquor store where customers wheel around enormous carts—the type they use in factories to move pieces of sheet metal—and fill them with half-gallon bottles of no-frills vodka. At six dollars a bottle, the bottles dance off the shelves. Beer and soda, which customers fetch themselves, are kept in walk-in refrigerators. In exchange for a discount, customers would unload a delivery, which they practically do anyway, to get to the liquor quicker. The only thing the customers don't do—and you have to admire their restraint—is drink the stuff on the spot.

There aren't many bars in the Valley. Drinking is more of a home scene. That's why they have all those liquor palaces the size of department stores. Supermarkets in the Valley aren't as big as the liquor stores, and half the sections at the supermarkets are stocked with booze. You get the impression that these people don't drink socially, that they're real alcoholics. People would rather stay home and drink in the privacy of their own despair.

For the most part they live in trailer parks or tract homes. In just a few years an entire population of technocrats, assembly-line workers, and get-rich schemers was superimposed on the previous population of farmers, small businessmen, professors from nearby Stanford University and San Jose State, and commuters from San Francisco. The Valley was a bedroom community with no real industry. That's why Highway 280 was built—because it gets you here fast. Now there's an indigenous population of factory workers—Chicanos, Orientals, blacks, and poor whites—and they and the farmers, small businessmen, professors, and the guys who've invested heavily in a product that might be obsolete before it gets out the door, are doing the drinking.

There's a lot of tension in the Valley. The factory workers get paid the least. They live in endless lines of tacky apartment buildings. There are the beautiful homes up in the hills with the pool and the view, but since business in the Valley is expanding much faster than housing, the tacky apartments rent for a fortune. Along one side of the Lawrence Expressway are endless factories and warehouses, and on the other side, behind corrugated tin walls, are rows of trailer parks. And these aren't fly-by-night parks. Mobile homes cost about thirty thousand dollars. The electronics industry is booming, and as it expands, guys with the mobile homes can move along with it. A year or two ago the microelectronics industry was mostly in the Valley. Now it's all over the country, and eventually the importance of the Valley will diminish—which is the way it happened in Detroit. With Detroit it took forty years. Here it will take two years.

*   *   *

One thing found in the Valley that resembles nothing on a chip is palm trees, particularly the two in Sunnyvale that stand majestically outside the community center in Murphy Park. They are all that is left of the Michael Murphy, Jr., estate, which he called Bayview, back when it was possible to see the bay from here.

Murphy's house was one of the first frame houses in California. The others were adobe or thatched. It was prefabricated in Bangor, Maine, shipped around the Horn, floated down the bay, and reassembled here. In the 1950s, when the town was renovated, the city fathers didn't want an old, rundown firetrap around.

At the time a bill declaring the house a landmark was about to be passed in Sacramento, but the bulldozers got there first. The community center was built in its place.

Howard Winters, one of the few Valley natives, and his wife are volunteer historians at the Sunnyvale Historical Society's museum, which occupies a corner of the center. Mr. Winters lives a half block from where he was born in 1936. When he grew up, the Valley was called "The Valley of the Heart's Delight." It's as if some strangers moved into his house and replaced the old familiar furniture with new, modular stuff.

HOWARD WINTERS: The Murphys started out as a poor Irish family. Times were bad in Ireland, so the Murphys went to Quebec. Times were bad in Quebec, so the Murphys went to Missouri. In Missouri they met this priest who was going to California. They joined his wagon train—a very important wagon train because it was the first wagon train that successfully went over the Sierra. Before that, they went around the mountains, either north or south.

Michael Murphy, Jr., settled in Sacramento where, around the time of the Gold Rush, he became a successful farmer, selling cattle and wheat to the miners. His father lived in San Jose. On one of his visits to his father, he decided to move from Sacramento and settle here. In 1851 he bought what is now Sunnyvale from Mariano Castro, who founded what is now Mountain View. Murphy's estate extended from Castro Street in Mountain View to the Law-rence Expressway in Sunnyvale and from the bay to El Camino Real in the west.

*   *   *

The first technology to roll into the Valley was the railroad. The railroad wanted to build a main line from San Francisco to San Jose, which would cross Murphy's property. Murphy gave the railroad the right of way in exchange for two stops—Murphy Station, where the Sunnyvale Station is now, and Lawrence Station—plus a free ride to any one of his prop-erties in California.

Some of Murphy's wheat went into making the original San Francisco steam beer, until he discovered that growing fruit trees was more profitable. Michael Murphy was one of the biggest and most popular landowners in the state. When his friends wanted to celebrate his fiftieth wedding anni-versary with a big barbecue, Murphy protested that it would be too exclusive and invited the entire state of California. It was the biggest event ever held in California history. The party ended two years later, when Murphy died.

HOWARD WINTERS: Most of Murphy's estate went to his heirs and to W.E. Crossman, an early Valley developer who married into the family. In the early 1900s Crossman put two hundred acres up for development. At the time there was just Murphy Station and Bayview Ranch. The big towns in the area were Mountain View and San Jose. Sunnyvale *was just a stage and train stop. What gave the town its big boost was the 1906 earthquake. Many industries had their buildings leveled in San Francisco, and Crossman promised them land with access to the railroad at $150 an acre if they relocated to Sunnyvale. The same acres go for half a million dollars today.*

Jubilee, makers of the "Cadillac of incubators," was the first manufacturer to take up the offer. Sunnyvale was hoping to develop a poultry industry to rival Petaluma; Jubilee was to be the incubator company that would service them. Then came Hendy Ironworks, which is now owned by Westinghouse, and Libby's, which, by combining bits and pieces of fruit left on the assembly line, invented fruit cocktail. At one time Libby's was the largest cannery in the world under one roof. Now it looks as if it will be redeveloped out of existence.

The first high technology to come to the Valley, and the turning point in its history, actually floated in in 1933, when the government commissioned Moffett Field to service a new fleet of dirigibles. This was before radar. The mother ship hid in the clouds, and little planes inside the dirigible would fly out in search of enemy shipping and report back. The dirigible *Macon* arrived at Moffett Field in 1933 and crashed in 1935. That was the end of the Navy's dirigible program but not the end of Moffett Field, which drew in Aries, Lockheed, the wind tunnel, and later NASA. During the Second World War the defense companies and the town prospered, but after the war they lost their contracts. The Chamber of Commerce, fearing the city would turn into a ghost town, pushed the development button. Land was cheap and so was labor. The weather was terrific. The Chamber of Commerce set up a big circus tent and industry came in, and the orchards came down. They shook the trees, and some say they shook too hard.

*   *   *

The Computer Age began during the Second World War. There had been early attempts at building a computer in the 1800s—Charles Babbage made an all-mechanical digital computer—but, for its size (about as big as four breadboxes), the computer didn't do very much. Before World War II there were knitting machines, adding machines, and calculators, which are a kind of computer but "dedicated," they do only what they're designed to do. It wasn't until the war that people started thinking seriously about building a digital computer that could be programmed to perform different functions.

Even as the Germans were amassing troops on the Polish border, they had an "Enigma machine," a box with which they could send and receive coded messages. They built up their army knowing that they were going to use this machine on a large scale. Rommel drove along the Polish border in his command car with one of the machines built into it, like a car radio, sending codes back and forth through the military system. Other countries' armies had to string phone wire because broadcast communications could be intercepted by enemies. All the German officer had to do was hit one key and the machine would transpose a message into a secret code which could be broadcast, or so they thought, without risk of interception. Meanwhile, inside Poland there were three Polish scientists who happened to possess one of these Enigma machines (which had probably been captured from the Germans), but they didn't know how to use it. The scientists smuggled it out of Poland and brought it to the British, who were in a better position to do something with it. The British built the first real computer at Benchley Park in London. Its purpose was to decipher the German code. The first one was built with vacuum tubes and programmed with paper tape, which looked like a piano roll.

Churchill knew the Germans planned to invade Poland months before they actually did because the British intercepted the Germans' military wireless traffic for the entire war. They knew that D-Day would succeed, although most history books say it was hit-or-miss. The Allies built up a phony landing force aimed at Calais. The British knew Hitler had gone for the bluff and sent his armies away from Normandy to Calais.

Since World War II the government has put up huge sums of money to develop technology. Usually when there's major advance in technology, it has some connection with defense. In the late sixties and seventies it had to do with the space program. When it comes to doing things in a big way, no one beats the government.

The best engineers and physicists wanted to work for the government—not out of patriotism or because the job paid well but for the opportunity to work with the best and latest technology that only the government had. It's always a kick to do the best job you can and go as far as you can without worrying whether some other company will develop a product first or whether, after spending all that money, you'll be able to sell it. There is absolutely no concern for that with government.

By the end of the war, IBM, Burroughs, and some other companies realized computers could be used in business. Computers were starting to be affordable enough for a very large business to buy one—although not affordable by any other standard. These computers took up an enormous space and had water pipes running through them. The vacuum tubes gave off so much heat that they actually had to be cooled with water. It was a common problem among certain computers for the pipes to break. Tubes also used an enormous amount of power. The power distribution wires were enormous. It was the big stuff you'd expect to find underground in New York City; cables so thick you couldn't put your hand around one.

In certain computers, like ENIAC, the most advanced computer for its day, the CPU (central processing unit), where all the data passes through and the numerical operations on data are done, was a room the size of a walk-in freezer. It was a huge computer, but it could handle only about twenty numbers simultaneously, which is not a lot considering its size. It didn't have much memory and wasn't particularly fast, yet it cost millions of dollars. Primitive as it was, it was faster than anything else around. It could do

ZAP!

mathematical equations in a couple of hours that a person couldn't do in a lifetime. It would have been totally impossible to put anything into orbit or to send a rocket to the moon as elegantly as they did without it. If NASA wanted to send something up, it wouldn't be on finesse. Without computers, they would have had to build rockets that would almost have to be driven like a car so that if it went a little bit off course it could be steered back on course, like Buck Rogers flying around space, steering his rocket like a van. Fortunately, that's not how things turned out.

*   *   *

In 1947 Dr. William Shockley and two colleagues at Bell Laboratories made a spectacular breakthrough in computer technology when they replaced the bulky and expensive vacuum tubes with a small, inexpensive device called a transistor. A transistor, about one one-hundredth the size of a tube, is basically a combination of compounds and elements that, when put together in a certain way, allows a small current to control a large current. A transistor is like a valve, where one current is a knob and the other is water flowing through the valve. A small turn of the knob controls the big movement of water. Although he shared a Nobel Prize for his part in inventing the transistor, Dr. Shockley will probably be best remembered either for his theory about blacks being genetically inferior to whites or for his contribution to a sperm bank dedicated to fathering future geniuses.

The reason Silicon Valley is in Santa Clara Valley and

12

not in San Fernando Valley or Sun Valley or Death Valley or Valley Stream, is because Dr. William Shockley's mom lived in Palo Alto, not far from Hewlett's garage. This is where Dr. Shockley went in 1954 after winning the Nobel Prize. Shockley, who was more entrepreneurially minded than his colleagues, wanted to find a way to cash in on this new invention. He received backing from Arnold Beckman of Beckman Instruments, a Southern Californian firm, somewhat comparable to Hewlett-Packard, and he invited a dozen top Ph.D.'s in physics and chemistry from around the country to a warehouse in Mountain View, where he set up Shockley Semiconductor. The product he wanted to commercialize was a three-layer diode, which he thought would be an improvement over the transistor. He was totally wrong. Within a year, eight of the hand-picked recruits, realizing the company was going nowhere, left for Fairchild Camera and Instrument, and in 1957, with Fairchild backing, they founded Fairchild Semiconductor, the Valley's first successful semiconductor company. In 1960 Beckman gave up on Shockley Semiconductor and sold it to Clevite of Cleveland, which in turn sold it to ITT, which didn't even try to unload it. They simply folded it. Shockley wasn't successful as a businessman, but he certainly was a good judge of talent.

Fairchild engineers, meanwhile, developed a smaller transistor and were able to fit a lot more of them into a package than Shockley could into his. As transistors became smaller and cheaper to make, and the demand became greater, more and more engineers left Fairchild to form their own companies. Dozens of semiconductor companies in the Valley, including the big three—National Semiconductor, Intel, and Advanced Microdevices—were started by rebellious Fairchildren. Had it not been for Shockley, however, there would be no Silicon Valley, and Nolan Bushnell would never have invented the video game.

2

NOLAN BUSHNELL was born in 1943 and grew up in Clearfield, Utah, near the Great Salt Lake. He was a Mormon. His father was a cement contractor whose motto was, "Work hard, play hard." Nolan remembers *Spin and Marty* on T.V. and never missed *Mr. Wizard* on Saturday afternoons. He was a ham radio operator; W7DUK were his call letters. His first enterprise was a washing machine-TV-radio repair business.

Nolan did well in school. He went to science fairs with dumb little things like voice-activated switches. He was a first-rate prankster. One night he attached a light bulb to a giant kite and fooled some of the local citizens into believing they were being invaded by aliens. He was six foot four by the seventh grade. He was good in sports but not great—very tall but awkward. He was on the school basketball team, usually riding the bench. Coaches said that with his height,

as soon as Nolan got his coordination, he would be a dy-
namite athlete. He's still waiting. Nolan always thought of
himself as a Renaissance man more than an engineer or
businessman. He was an all-state debator in high school.
He took as many courses in philosophy at the University of
Utah as he did in math.

Nolan spent most nights in the school's computer lab,
playing a computer game engineering students have been
playing in computer labs since 1962, when an MIT student
named Steve Russell wrote the program called Spacewar.
Nolan lost his tuition in a poker game one night, and he
spent the next two summers working on the midway of an
amusement park, guessing people's weights or manning a
booth where, for a quarter, someone got three chances to
knock over some milk bottles with a baseball. He envisioned
the midway one day lined with coin-operated computer
games. Mainframe computers like the ones at school cost
millions of dollars, weighed many tons, and would never fit
through a door. It would take a lot of quarters just to break
even, so Nolan put his brainstorm on the back burner.

He received his degree in engineering in 1968. A year
later he and his wife, whom he'd married in 1967, moved
to California. Nolan got a ten-thousand-dollar-a-year job as
a research design engineer in the computer graphics department of Ampex Corporations, one of the high-tech
companies to land in Sunnyvale when the Chamber of
Commerce shook the trees. Nolan's first choice was to work
for Disney, but they weren't hiring engineers straight out of
school. He settled for Ampex because it was in California,
where the action was.

The Rise and Fall of Atari

After work Nolan drives from Ampex on Kiser Road, near the Central Expressway, north on the Lawrence Expressway to Stevens Creek Boulevard. He lives in a development where you can live in one of four cities, depending on which side of the street you are on. Nolan is on the Santa Clara corner—there's his house now, three bedrooms with family room in Gibson Court, where he lives with his wife, Paula, and their two daughters, and there's a light on in the bedroom.

It is 4 A.M. in 1970. Nolan's daughter is sleeping on the sofa in the living room because her father has converted her bedroom into a minicomputer lab. Twenty-seven-year-old Nolan is tangled in a maze of wires, getting the bugs out of a computer game he's inventing by hooking up a nineteen-inch black and white G.E. television set to 185 commercial integrated circuits, mostly of the transistor-transistor logic (TTL) variety. The game, dubbed Computer Space, in which a dogfight between a spaceship and flying saucers takes place in deep space, is a knockoff of Spacewar. Texas Instruments has come out with the 7400 series TTL, which has made it possible for him to buy a minicomputer that interfaces with his game for under forty thousand dollars, and the price is falling. He had his name on a purchase order but canceled it just before he decided he would build his own computer. That's when he kicked his daughter out of her bedroom.

The minicomputer around which Nolan first attempted to build Computer Space was smart enough to calculate the pull of gravity on a rocketship orbiting a planet but couldn't display it graphically on an inexpensive TV screen.

17

ZAP!

Nolan had to design fairly complex and extensive circuitry just to get those crummy rockets that looked like boxes up on the screen. Nolan began to realize that this kludge was not going to be the small and inexpensive package he needed to make the first successful commercial video game. Then he had a breakthrough. What if, instead of a minicomputer, he built a fixed-purpose game-playing machine? It would never calculate pi to 1,024 places or handle accounts receivable for a medium-sized company. All it would do is play Computer Space, which was all Nolan wanted it to do. So the minicomputer was shoved under the bed, and the game plan for all first-generation video games, like Space Invaders, Asteroids, and Pac-Man, was conceived.

Meanwhile, in another part of the Valley, Bill Pitts—who played Spacewar at Stanford—using a Digital Equipment Corp. PDP-11 computer was inventing a commercial version of Spacewar of his own called Galaxy Game. Pitt's game was very similar to Nolan's but not as cost-effective.

* * *

According to Ralph Baer, the Tom Edison of video games, the first video game had already been invented. Baer married the computer to the TV set in 1966, before Nolan ever conceived of Computer Space, but it was kept under wraps for a number of years.

Baer, who had fled from the Nazis in Germany, where he was born, was working at Sanders Associates in New Hampshire, supervising a staff of 500 engineers and technicians, when he built a game console that could be attached to an ordinary home TV set. What's interesting is that Sanders is a highly sophisticated military systems consulting firm. Why were they interested in home video games in 1966? It was as if the Pentagon had decided to put out a line of soft ice cream on the side.

Baer built a couple of symbol generators, and when he succeeded in getting two spots to chase each other around a black and white screen, he hired Bill Harrison and Bill Rusch to work full-time on the top-secret TV game project. They worked in a ten-by-fifteen-foot windowless office called the "game room," which had two desks, a workbench, and auxiliary electronics equipment. The door was always locked, and only Baer and the two Bills had the key. Since the two engineers loved to play recorded electronic guitar music while they worked, the other employees figured they were developing some kind of electronic guitar. Within a year they had a working ball-and-paddle game, which, six months later, they developed into a sophisticated video hockey game. In 1969, when Nolan started at Ampex, Baer was wooing Teleprompter, RCA, Zenith, G.E., Magnavox, and other television technology companies to license his video game concept. He and RCA played footsie for six months. RCA pulled out at the last moment, when Sanders Associates refused to be owned by RCA as part of the deal. Meanwhile Bill Enders, from the RCA negotiating team, joined Magnavox and got them interested in licensing Baer's idea. A secret deal was struck in 1970, just as Nolan was starting to build Computer Space.

ZAP!

* * *

The true hero of this story is neither Nolan Bushnell nor Ralph Baer, but something smaller than a fingernail. It looks like a square contact lens and is as fragile as a soap bubble yet all of Atari is built on it. It's called an integrated circuit, popularly known as a microchip, and the future of technology rests on its minuscule shoulders.

The first microchip was created at Fairchild by Robert Noyce, one of Shockley's original engineers. Chips are made of silicon, after oxygen, the most abundant element, on earth. Silicon is special because it has the properties of a semiconductor: by itself, it neither conducts electricity, as does metal, nor insulates, as does rubber; but with the addition of certain chemicals, it can behave like either. Printed on this silicon speck are thousands of tiny on-off switches called transistors. The transistors are etched into the chip through a process similar to photo silkscreening, except the pattern is microscopic. The silicon substrate is extremely thin, and by stacking different circuits one on top of another, a fairly complex structure can be built. By hooking up some fairly complex structures to a common TV set, Nolan Bushnell invented the first commercial video game.

As chip technology became more sophisticated, so did video games. As chip manufacturers learned to make smaller and smaller masks (screens) and etched finer and finer lines on smaller substrates, the chips got smarter and the games faster. As the circuits operated faster, the resolution on the screen became sharper. As the dots on the screen got denser, the graphics looked more realistic. More dots could mean more colors. As video games became more popular, they showcased the newest technological innovations.

*   *   *

Steve Bristow was a typical engineering student at Berkeley in the riot years, 1968–1969. He didn't wear bellbottoms or love beads. He walked around campus with a dozen pens and pencils in a nerd pack in his shirt pocket. He didn't riot. He didn't demonstrate, protest, sit in, or freak out. He certainly didn't drop acid. Bristow was in a program in which he went to classes for six months and worked in the field six months. He had interviews with a few companies and ended up working at Ampex.

STEVE BRISTOW: The guy I was assigned to was Nolan Bushnell. That was during my freshman year, from September 1969 to March 1970. When I returned to Ampex in 1971, Nolan had come up with this idea for an electronic game and was working on the prototype. I didn't know exactly what it was he was working on but I knew it wasn't what the rest of us were working on. By spring the model was nearly finished, and Nolan left Ampex and went to Nutting Associates, an obscure coin-operated-game manufacturer who had hit with an IQ game. He planned to develop his electronic game to completion there and sell the manufacturing rights to Nutting.

ZAP!

To get to Nutting, Nolan took either El Camino Real or Stevens Creek to Highway 85, depending upon traffic. While he still lived with his wife, he drove a Buick station wagon or a VW convertible. When he and his wife split up—he was spending too much time working on Computer Space and not enough time with the family—Paula kept the Bug and Nolan the station wagon. When Nolan went to Nutting, he took along Ted Dabney, his roommate at Ampex.

STEVE BRISTOW: During lunch hours a few of us would drive over from Ampex to Nolan's lab at Nutting, where he had bits and pieces of the game working. Then I went back to school. By the end of the winter quarter 1972, the local economy had fallen apart, and the job I was returning to at Ampex evaporated with layoffs. So I phoned Nolan over at Nutting and went to work there. By this time Nolan had licensed Computer Space to Nutting, and the game was already in production.

Most people in the coin-operated-game business had never seen a computer game before. Their field was pinball, skee-ball, and jukeboxes and they were skeptical.

Nutting built 1,500 Computer Space games and, as company president Bill Nutting tells it, they had to sell some at gunpoint. Nolan felt Nutting was screwing up the marketing: "I felt I wouldn't be successful if I was burdened by the Nutting management." Nolan and Bill got into a fight in May 1972, and Nolan quit.

Computer Space didn't sell well for the same reason

The Rise and Fall of Atari

Bill Pitts' Galaxy didn't: It was too complex. Nolan was sure a high-technology product like a computer game should have a high-tech theme, so he gambled that Computer Space was the right game to commercialize. It wasn't until Computer Space bombed that Nolan realized the problem.

NOLAN BUSHNELL: You had to read the instructions before you could play, people didn't want to read instructions. To be successful, I had to come up with a game people already knew how to play; something so simple that any drunk in any bar could play.

*   *   *

Nolan, Ted Dabney, and Larry Bryan, another engineer from Ampex, agreed to put up $100 each and set up their own computer game business. The three sat around Nolan's house one night, trying to come up with a name for their new company. Larry, thumbing through the dictionary, came up with *syzygy*, meaning the straight-line configuration of three celestial bodies. Nolan looked at Ted, who looked at Larry, and Syzygy it was. When it came to anteing, however, Larry dropped out. Nolan and Ted more than made up for this and kicked in $250 each. Larry Bryan, now just a footnote in Atari history, is probably still kicking himself.

Nolan applied for the name Syzygy, but a roofing company in California already had that name. Bushnell and Dabney played around with B.D., Inc. and D.B., Inc., but those names sounded too much like Black and Decker or

ZAP!

Dunn and Bradstreet. At the time Nolan was playing a lot of the Japanese game go, and it occurred to him to list his three favorite go expressions—*sente*, the equivalent of "checkmate" in chess; *atari*, which means "check"; and *hanne*, the word used to acknowledge an overtaking move. Somebody in the office of the California Secretary of State liked the second name best, and on June 27, 1972, Atari was officially incorporated.

3

ATARI'S first location, 2962 Scott Boulevard, in the low-rent district of Santa Clara, was a typical industrial park with a lot of small-office-type spaces, twenty or thirty feet at the front and going back maybe a hundred feet.

It was 1972. Al Alcorn, Atari's first full-time engineer, who was earning fourteen or fifteen thousand dollars a year, was in the lab poking around inside a computer with a wire that was hooked up to a speaker. On the other side of the country, five plumbers were breaking into the Democratic National Headquarters in the Watergate office building. Nolan had an idea for a simple video game any drunk could play and Al was putting together the not-so-simple circuitry. Al was an engineering whiz from Berkeley who had replaced Nolan at Ampex when Nolan went to Nutting. Nolan could have built the game himself, but he was working on the two-man version of Computer Space that Nutting had commissioned. Nolan really wanted to build a driving game, but since Al was new at building video games, Nolan was starting him off with a paddle game that was less complicated.

There were basically two types of computers that Al could build the game around, analogue and digital. Minicomputers, mainframes, pocket calculators, microwave oven controls, and most of what are commonly thought of as computers are digital. The automatic throttle found on some automobiles is analogue. An analogue computer uses voltage or current to represent numeric quantities. Two volts might stand for the number two. It can perform one function only, but it performs this function instantaneously. When two wires, each carrying five volts, enter an analogue computer, ten volts leave. When two and three volts enter, five volts leave. The analogue computer *is* the mathematical equation. The solution is instantaneous, whether adding a million numbers or two.

Quantities in digital computers are represented by a pattern of voltages in one of two states: on or off. This system of on-off is known as binary representation. Digital calculation is sequential, not instantaneous like analogue, and because it works in stages, a computer's function can be changed by reordering the sequence of operations rather than by rewiring the circuit.

There was no computer per se in the video game Al was building, just a few TTL logic chips, mostly digital circuitry. The game was based on dedicated logic. Al built a separate circuit for each function: one for the paddles, one for the score, one for the ball. The black and white picture on the screen was a graphic representation of the changing on and off patterns in the circuitry.

The image on the screen, as on all television screens, was generated by a technology known as raster scan: An electron beam, independent of the desired image's shape, moves across the screen in a serpentine pattern, first horizontally, then down a little, then across again, and so on until the beam has swept the entire screen. When Al wanted to move the position of his paddle, he rotated a knob to change the current that controlled the vertical position of the dots on the screen that formed the paddle. Both paddles and ball were made of phosphorescent light but each behaved differently. The position of the ball was determined by a computer. The electron beam was running across and down the screen all the time. The paddles and ball were not really there at the same time (nor, for that matter, are any two images on a raster-generated TV screen)—it was an illusion that they were. Phosphors stay lit for quite a long time, for just as the light dies down, the beam comes around again.

To move the ball on the screen, Al had to keep track of four things: the horizontal position of the beam, the vertical position of the beam, and the desired horizontal and vertical positions of the ball. If he wanted to put the ball on top of the screen, he had to wait for the TV beam to get there. He could tell which line the beam was on and where along the line it was because he had built a series of four-bit counters that counted the lines. It is a digital counter that is "bumped" every time there is a pulse that wants the counter to advance—about sixteen thousand bumps per second.

The image on the screen was a pattern made up of dark and light areas. The lightness and darkness were controlled by patterns of on and off states within the circuit. Since the patterns were changing, and since the patterns were made up of changing voltages, wave forms were generated that, when amplified and sent through a speaker, produced various tones.

Nolan had described to Al the sound he wanted the game to have by putting his thumb against the inside of his cheek and popping it out. Nolan wanted the hollow, ringing sound of a one-and-one-half-inch polyvinyl chloride pipe striking a tennis ball. Al was auditioning a number of these sounds for Nolan when, *pong*, he found it. It was a tick in the vertical line counter, amplified. To the ears of the two engineers it was planetary music.

The dictionary defines "pong" as a hollow, ringing sound. Nolan called his electronic game Pong because Ping-Pong was already copyrighted.

*   *   *

The regulars, mostly college and post-college kids, filed into Andy Capp's, a local bar in Sunnyvale. After coming in from the bright California sunlight, Andy Capp's seemed very dark. It took a moment for their eyes to focus. First they saw the familiar purple fluorescent light of the jukebox, then the blinking lights of the pinball machine, and then a strange blue-gray light from a TV game they had never seen before. It looked something like a booth at an arcade, but instead of a gypsy, there was a blip bouncing around a trapezoidal screen, reminiscent of the doorways on *Star Trek*. Instead of flipper buttons like those on pinball machines, there were two knobs.

One of the regulars approached the Pong game inquisitively and studied the ball bouncing silently around the screen as if in a vacuum. A friend joined him. The instructions said: "Avoid missing ball for high score." One of the kids inserted a quarter. There was a beep. The game had begun. They watched dumbfoundedly as the ball appeared alternately on one side of the screen and then dissappeared on the other. Each time it did the score changed. The score was tied at 3–3 when one player tried the knob controlling the paddle at his end of the screen. The score was 5–4, his favor, when his paddle made contact with the ball. There was a beautifully resonant "pong" sound, and the ball bounced back to the other side of the screen. 6–4. At 8–4 the second player figured out how to use his paddle. They had their first brief volley just before the score was 11–5 and the game was over.

Seven quarters later they were having extended volleys, and the constant pong noise was attracting the curiosity of others at the bar. Before closing, everybody in the bar had played the game. The next day people were lined up outside Andy Capp's at 10 A.M. to play Pong. Around ten o'clock that night, the game suddenly died.

ZAP!

Less than forty-eight hours after Atari had installed the Pong test model in Andy Capp's, there was a call at Atari for Nolan. Nolan was in Chicago, showing Pong to Bally's Midway, a giant coin-operated-games business, so Al Alcorn took the call. "The fucking machine's broken. Get it out of here," a bartender at Andy Capp's screamed. Al drove over to Andy Capp's to look at the game's circuitry. The place was a mess from the night before and it stank of stale beer. Al opened the front panel of the machine with his key and threw the credit switch on the coin mechanism, which allowed him to play without paying. The game worked perfectly. He deduced immediately that the problem was not in the circuitry but that the coin mechanism was broken. He released the latch on the coin mechanism. Inside, the maze the coin traveled down looked like an ant colony clogged with quarters. The game wasn't broken; the sawed-off plastic milk container they were using as a coin box had to be emptied.

*   *   *

Nolan opened his briefcase, took out a portable unit of Pong Al had made, and showed it to two astonished executives who ran Bally's Midway. He was trying to sell the concept of Pong to them to manufacture. Nolan stood to make more money if he manufactured Pong himself, but that involved the cost of materials, machinery, bigger facilities, more employees. He preferred to build one prototype and move on to the next project. Nolan had approached Nutting with

Pong first, but Nutting didn't like the royalties Nolan was offering. The two execs at Midway weren't interested, either. Like the other coin-operated-game manufacturers he had showed his electronic game to, they were still in the electromechanical era, of which pinball is a prime example.

The basic moving parts in a pinball game are the bumpers, which are controlled by electromagnets called solenoids. When a ball lands in a bumper—the things in the little circles that light up that are worth a certain amount of points—the movement of the ball against the bumper throws a switch that energizes the solenoid; the solenoid throws the bumper back, which shoots the ball in whichever direction the bumper is pointed. The score is kept by a mechanical counter; every time the solenoid is energized, it advances the counter one count.

The ones wheel has a little cam on it so that every time it comes around it kicks over the tens wheel, which in turn has a cam on it that kicks over the hundreds wheel, and so on. Pinball companies make pinball bumpers, flippers, solenoids, relays, and mechanical scorers, and Nolan was coming to them with an idea for a game with just two moving parts—and both were identical. Pong had no tilt, clickity-clack sound, bells, or place to put a drink. There was nothing in Nolan's game that interested these executives—video games were simply not in their field of expertise. Nolan went back to his hotel and phoned Al, but before he could tell him the bad news, Al was ranting about Pong's success at Andy Capp's. That was when Nolan decided to manufacture Pong himself.

* * *

While taking Pong around to coin-operated-game manufacturers, Nolan had also dropped in on various coin-op-game distributors to get their reactions to Pong as well as a better feel for the market. Distributors buy games from the manufacturers and either sell or lease them, on a percentage basis, to operators who put the machines out on the street. One of the first distributors Nolan saw was Ira Bettelman of C.A. Robinson in Los Angeles, a major pinball and rifle-game distributor since the 1930s.

IRA BETTELMAN: Nolan was the kind of guy our industry needed. He was a creative, avant-garde, talented, highly qualified engineer who achieved his fantasy with no business savvy. At the time we got hold of Pong, we were representing ten or twelve coin-operated-game manufacturers and didn't think too much of Pong as a machine. Obviously we were experts in our field, and here comes something we knew nothing about, weren't prepared for, and didn't know what to do with. It was a culture-shocking event. We have a saying in this business, "The only thing that counts is what's in the cashbox." Regardless of our prejudices or fears of the unknown, we put the Pong machine out in the field with one of our customers and quickly found out that the returns were astronomical. How quickly? In a matter of *a week. In this business you always find out quickly. The cashbox in the original Pong was a bread pan—a pan used to bake bread in, which held up to 1,200 quarters, or $300. When the game was in a good location, this pan took about a week to fill.*

*   *   *

Nolan leased pinball games from other manufacturers, some of whom he tried to sell Pong to as a way of generating money to develop Pong. These pinball machines cost virtually nothing down and more than covered their monthly installments. With the combined incomes from pinball, a few outside consulting jobs, and a fifty-thousand-dollar line of credit on receivables from Wells Fargo bank, Nolan set out to manufacture Pong.

He rented some space a few blocks from Atari's Scott Boulevard headquarters, on Martin Avenue in Santa Clara, in what had been a roller skating rink and still had nice hardwood floors and set up manufacturing facilities. He hired some hippies to work on the production line. At first Nolan and Al Alcorn worked alongside them, assembling Pongs for twelve to sixteen hours a day for next to no pay. On good days they got ten machines out the door. The average life of the normal coin-operated game was three months.

Atari shipped their first Pong in November 1972 and had Pongs working through most of 1973, when they moved their main facilities to Winchester Boulevard, Santa Clara.

ZAP!

In 1973 a good production run for a pinball game was 3,000 units; Pong started with a run of 2,500. In all, Atari produced over 8,000. The top arcade game of the day, the very best, collected $45 a week; Pong brought in $200 a week, 8,000 quarters weighing nearly 100 pounds—enough to give Steve Bristow a hernia.

WHILE Nolan was running the day-to-day operation at Atari, Steve Bristow was earning his keep at Berkeley, running the arcade route, servicing and collecting money from the 100 Pong, Computer Space, and pinball machines Atari operated there, earning 1 percent of the gross. He took his trusty coin-counting machine with him along the route, and when the coins were counted, he gave half to the operator. Besides Berkeley, which was Bristow's route, Atari had other local arcade routes in Santa Clara County they distributed themselves. These were handy for testing new games. When Ted Dabney left the company in 1973, he ended up running some of the routes.

Upon graduating from college, Bristow interviewed with various companies and received the best job offer from Atari. An engineer fresh out of school had three choices for employment in 1973: Ampex, Lockheed, or Atari. Atari was the best thing happening.

ZAP!

When Bristow arrived in June 1973, many of the seventy or eighty people working for Atari were long-haired freaks, bikers and dropouts, who assembled wiring harnesses or soldered circuit boards. They were hired not for their skills but on the basis of their good vibes. There were a few accountants. Al Alcorn was in charge of engineering, and Bristow was made second in command. The rest of the department consisted of a few electrical engineers from Stanford, Berkeley, and Ampex. Their instructions from Nolan were to develop Pong-like games, and they came up with Pong Doubles, SuperPong, and Space Race.

STEVE BRISTOW: The way the coin-operated business worked at that time was by exclusivity. Distributors didn't share. One distributor sold only Gottlieb pinball, Wurlitzer jukeboxes, and someone else's shuffleboard. Another distributed Bally pinball, Seaberg jukeboxes, and somebody else's skeeball. Nolan wanted maximum distribution, so he created his own competition. He took his next-door neighbor, Joe Keenan, and set up an operation in the fall of 1973 called Kee Games, which was owned by Atari but appeared to distributors to be Atari's biggest competitor in video games.

One Saturday morning my wife kept the guard busy at the front door of Atari while I was throwing circuit boards and equipment out the window and Keenan was putting them into my car. Even though it was legal, we kept it secret.

I went to work at Kee Games. We started out with something called Elimination, a four-player table model Pong-type game that did so well Atari copied it. They came back with a version called Quadrapong. Out of the same factory Atari was producing competing circuit boards. Atari went through some ups and downs in management, and Kee kept going along until finally, in the fall of 1974, it was announced that Atari and Kee had merged. But before the announcement was made, Kee came out with a pretty attractive game called Tanks; attractive enough so that Kee's distributors and Atari's distributors no longer insisted on exclusivity. Nolan's scheme had worked.

Ira Bettelman, however, claims he knew Atari and Kee were the same company all along: "There are no secrets in this business."

*   *   *

What happened to Nolan Bushnell and Atari had happened a generation earlier to Arthur "Spud" Melin and Wham-O, a sporting goods mail order business he ran out of his garage in Southern California in the 1940s. Spud Melin didn't actually invent the Hula Hoop—some Australian aborigines did—but he made the first one out of plastic in the 1950s.

A friend of his had been to Australia and had heard that this rattan hoop was a hot item and had sold a million in a country with a population of ten million. His friend picked one up, brought it back to the U.S., and left it with Spud Melin but never told him what to do with it. Melin rolled it down the street. He threw it at stakes and wastepaper baskets and played horseshoes. Finally, in late 1957, he put

ZAP!

it in the storeroom. A toy manufacturer from Australia, tour-
ing the country, buying products to take back with him,
stopped by Wham-O. Melin got the rattan hoop out of the
storeroom and asked the Australian what to do with it. The
Australian gave a brief demonstration. The women blushed—
it was pretty risqué in those days. Wham-O started making
some out of rattan strips, then switched to plastic. At the
time high-density polyethylene was new on the market, and
no one had used it. They made up a few hoops and took
them around to stores. The toy trade didn't think it would
be successful. There were comments like, "You can't sell
a piece of used garden hose for two dollars." It was a unique,
amazing thing in those days. Melin filed for a patent, of
course, but he wasn't waiting two years for one to be issued.
Once he started the ball rolling, he couldn't stop.

Melin set up several plants with 500 employees working two shifts making nothing but hoops. It was very close
to the end of the season, however, and the reps thought
they might be too late. Then the hoop was featured on the
Dinah Shore Chevy Show, and that kicked the product across
the country. Sales skyrocketed. There were Hula Hoop par-
ties, Hula Hoop weddings, and Hula Hoop songs. It was the
thing to do that year, 1958. The demand was incredible.
Wham-O tried to stay on top of it the best they could. The
top production day was 100,000 hoops. It didn't last long,
however, because they didn't have a patent. A hoop is a
simple thing to make—anyone with an extruder and some
plastic could make one. Soon the country was flooded with
hoops.

The Rise and Fall of Atari

Likewise, anyone with a computer and a television set could make a Pong game, and almost everyone who had both did. Pong was in the field less than three months when companies like Midway, Allied Leisure, Ramtek, and Nutting came out with Pong look-alikes.

There were countless companies. Fly-by-night operations were building five games a week in their garages and selling them to their brothers-in-law. According to *Fortune* magazine, of the hundred thousand Pong-type games produced in 1974, only a tenth were made by Atari. Ira Bettelman thinks Atari sold a hell of a lot more than ten thousand. Steve Bristow puts the figure around 25 percent. It wasn't exactly what he would call fair competition, though: "Assuming everybody had similar production costs, Atari's profit margin was the lowest, because the others weren't supporting the engineering to develop their game. Atari was." Nonetheless, Atari squeezed out $3.2 million in earnings for fiscal 1973. Atari could have cornered the video game market, just as Wham-O could have cornered the hoop market, had they had the production capital. But by the time Atari received a patent and trademark, Pong was, like the Hula Hoop, already obsolete.

IRA BETTELMAN: There were certain advantages to having all those imitators. If Atari had had the market to itself, Pong and its derivatives—SuperPong, Pong Doubles, Quadra-Pong, Space Race, and Gotcha—would have lasted a year, maybe two years or longer. But, because there were so many companies in the business trying to do so many variations of the same game, all at the same time, Pong was exhausted in six months. We realized very quickly that unless Atari offered us something new and different, they weren't going to match the success of the original Pong. We were a little concerned because we didn't want to see more than Pong for one, Pong for two, Pong for three, and Pong for four players. It was really getting monotonous. Somebody had to come up with the next generation in a hurry. Imagine if Wham-O had been the only one with a hoop. There would have been Singing Hula Hoops, hoops with flashing lights, hoops with streamers, and there would have been no end to it. Since mid-1973 we had been wondering if this was something that would go somewhere or if this was all these guys could do.

5

Is THERE life after Pong? The summer of 1974 was one of the most difficult periods in Nolan's life. Atari was severely undercapitalized and teetering on bankruptcy. Their biggest problem was that the company was always trying to grow to the limits of its resources. In 1973 they had set up Atari Japan to manufacture coin-operated games in Japan before most U.S. companies existed there, and they had lost their shirts. It wasn't because they were cash-poor or because they weren't doing it right but because they were using all their money to expand. They ended up losing half a million dollars, their profit for 1972.

After two years of any routine, most entrepreneurs move on to something new. At this point Nolan was an executive, not an engineer, and it gave Nolan a headache. According to the *Wall Street Journal*, people running small expanding companies suffered twice as much from tension as people running giant corporations.

ZAP!

Tidying up was not high on Nolan's list, but his office wasn't particularly messy. The calendar on his desk was divided up into video games instead of months. Dodgem, Frenzy, Pin Pong. It rained a lot during Touch-Me. Dr. Pong flew by, and before anyone knew it, it was Tank. Atari had put out a new game every six weeks just to cover expenses. They had to come up with fifteen game ideas for every four they developed. One of the games Nolan was counting on was Grantrak 10, the first video driving game. Although the game is a classic, production costs were so high and accounting costs so inadequate that it sold for $995 and cost $1,095 to build. With every unit they shipped, they shipped a hundred-dollar bill.

Meanwhile, downstairs, machines were going out untested, without coinboxes, with the wrong plugs. What really riled Nolan the most was that every day eight hundred dollars' worth of equipment was walking out the door. Nolan underestimated how many video games could fit inside the trunk of a car. According to one of the line workers wearing a "Fuck You" T-shirt, the pay was so bad, some workers felt compelled to steal.

LINE WORKER: I started working for Atari on day one, assembling harnesses and soldering circuit boards twelve or sixteen hours a day for $1.75 an hour. Two years later I was still doing the same shit for $1.75 an hour, while Nolan was sitting upstairs wearing that big bow tie of his, running a company that was worth $20 million with branches in Australia, Asia, Europe, South America, and who knows where else. They made a couple of buddies of mine supervisors and gave them a lousy fifty cents more an hour, but they weren't making any of them managers. We'd seen a lot of expensive help from the outside come into the company, but we didn't see more product going out.

NOLAN BUSHNELL: We were hiring people as fast as we could and paid them hippie wages, which was still above minimum wage. It was a situation where we were doing an awful lot of training. We were above scale in engineering and marketing. On production I think we lagged a little, but we had a no-layoff policy. We had some guys who should have been fired, but instead they weren't getting raises. There was a group of malcontents that tried to organize a union drive that we successfully fought. Because we were growing faster than we could train people, we had to bring in experienced people from the outside. But all employees received the same medical benefits as the executives. We had a special fund in the event of unwanted pregnancy. I hadn't made a penny running Atari. I was working for about twenty thousand dollars a year, which is subsistence.

The only people not griping were in the engineering department. The engineers weren't getting rich, but they were having a lot of fun playing and refining video games. Every so often Nolan and the top engineers and executives would grab a few kegs of beer and a bag of funny cigarettes and head off on what was euphorically called an R&D "retreat."

ZAP!

The future of any high-tech company is its R&D, which conceives and develops new ideas and products. A lot of Atari's best game ideas came out of these rip-roaring brainstorming bashes.

At first these retreats were held at a Holiday Inn for a day. In 1974 the site was often the Pajaro Dunes, a seaside condominium development where they rented a condo or two and forty people from Atari would come down. There were also informal planning sessions taking place over lunch, on airplanes, or at baseball games. The more private ones took place in hot tubs. Most strategy meetings in the Valley took place in hot tubs. Nolan had one at his new house in Los Gatos. There was also one in the engineering building. Nolan, Al Alcorn, Gene Lipkin, and Joe Keenan had one of these informal, private bull sessions in Nolan's Los Gatos hot tub in summer 1974.

Nolan was the tall guy with dark hair, not athletic, but not flabby. Al Alcorn, built like a football tackle, had dark hair and a full beard; the guys had nicknamed him Moose. Gene Lipkin also had a full dark beard, but he was taller, lankier. Gene was always in motion—sort of like Al, but he moved a lot faster. He was a boisterous, deep-voiced, back-slapping guy who had come over from Allied Leisure, one of the first companies to successfully knock off Pong, to become Atari's vice president of marketing. Gene's dad had been in the coin-operated-game business, and Gene was the only one at Atari with real marketing experience. The first thing Nolan told Gene when he joined the company was that they could keep going the way they were and live

44

well for the rest of their lives, or they could take a chance and go for the whole enchilada and maybe blow it. Nolan was an all-or-nothing type guy.

Joe Keenan, who was a year older than Nolan, was the only one in the pool who looked like he was over thirty. He had started out as a salesman for IBM. When he came to the depressing realization that he would never be president of the company, he left for a smaller one, Applied Logic. Then Nolan made him president of Kee Games, and after the merger Nolan made him president of Atari. By working his way down, Joe had reached the top. All four men had lots of charisma. Keenan, however, was more mellow and not as hard a charger as the others. Each had a very high tolerance for risk. All took chances and made snap decisions.

They were bobbing in the water, kicking around an idea for a game that Al was pushing. The best ideas in these sessions were given code names, usually after female employees, and Al's was "Darlene." Of all the female employees, Nolan remembers Darlene the best: "She was stacked and had the tiniest waist."

* * *

The difference between "Darlene" and all the Pongs before her was that you could take Darlene home and hook her up to the TV set. Darlene was Home Pong.

When Atari and Kee Games merged, Steve Bristow became vice president of engineering at Atari, and Al Alcorn, who didn't want to be vice president of engineering anymore, shifted to vice president of R&D, which researched and developed new ideas and future products. Now that Atari had a VP of R&D, they needed something for Al to do.

Al was hot to do a home video consumer product. He went to Harold Lee, an engineer at Atari, and asked him if it would be possible to compress a coin-operated game like Pong down to a few large-scale integrated (LSI) circuits that could hook up to a TV set at home. Lee thought it was possible. In the fall of 1974, Al started working on what turned out to be Home Pong, which was an improved version of Ralph Baer's Odyssey game.

Odyssey, the original home video game that Baer had developed and Magnavox had licensed through Sanders and put on the market in 1972, had over three hundred discrete parts. It came with hand controls, dice, playing cards, play money—twelve games in all. Plastic overlays, which were placed on the TV screen, provided the various playing fields. As primitive as Odyssey was, Magnavox sold 100,000 units at $100 each, the first year.

Home Pong was a dedicated game. It played only Pong, not twelve games like Odyssey. The LSI chips interfaced with an RF modulator, which interfaced with the television set. If you opened an original Home Pong you would find two or three LSI's and a few discrete components like transistors, capacitors, and conductors. Due to this new technology, Atari's resolution was far superior, the controls were more responsive and, because of the cheaper LSI chips, Pong cost less to produce and retailed for less than Odyssey.

The Rise and Fall of Atari

Atari was the only video game company to manufacture both coin-operated and home video games. Other companies with video games manufactured one or the other. Most of the twenty-seven or so "jackals," as Nolan called rival companies like Ramtek and Meadows Games that had Pong-like games, dropped out of the market. Atari's only major competitor was Bally's Midway, whose first video game effort was a non-Pong game called Gun Fight.

Midway had a big arcade hit in 1975–76 with a periscope game called Sea Wolf. A coin-op video game was considered a success when it sold five thousand units; Sea Wolf sold ten thousand. Atari's biggest game during this period, Tank, conceived by Bristow and put out by Kee Games in November 1974, carried Atari through 1975. It was followed by a slew of less impressive games like Tank II, Anti-Aircraft, and Jaws. Atari's only real competitor in the home video game market was Magnavox's Odyssey, whose sales by 1975 had reached $22 million. Magnavox, however, had lost $60 million because of Odyssey by the same year, for two reasons: their exclusive distributor didn't distribute to toy stores and from their advertising, customers thought the game worked only on a Magnavox TV set.

The reason no other company went into both the coin-operated video and home video game market was that they are two completely separate businesses, with different technologies, distribution networks, and markets. The manufacturing process is similar but requires new facilities. Starting a new, separate division devoted to consumer electronics ties up a considerable amount of cash (which

Atari didn't have) in inventory that wouldn't be sold until Christmas. Nolan's advisors and some top executives urged him against going into a new business. If he had been a good businessman he would have listened. But Nolan was not a good businessman. He had a gut feeling that Home Pong would succeed. In 1975 Nolan introduced Home Pong at the toy industry show. It sold out before it reached the stores.

*   *   *

One morning, a short time before the toy show opened, Tom Quinn, the sporting goods buyer—not the toy buyer—for Sears, Roebuck, showed up on Atari's doorstep in Los Gatos totally out of the blue and offered to buy every Home Pong game Atari could produce. Nolan told him he could produce only 75,000 units. Tom Quinn told Nolan to double production and he would arrange financing. In exchange, Sears wanted exclusive rights to sell Home Pong through its 900 outlets. And it would pay for advertising to boot. Nolan thought he was dreaming. Had Quinn showed up on Magnavox's doorstep and offered it the same deal, Atari probably would have gone under. Instead, Atari's sales by the end of 1975 were almost $40 million, with earnings between $2.5 million and $3.5 million.

Whenever the men in shirts and ties from Sears dropped by Atari, the technicians hid in the back room, for fear of alienating them. Bob Brown, an engineering supervisor at Atari, had just designed Video Music, a game that hooked up to the TV set and the stereo so that the sound from the stereo produced psychedelic visuals on the TV screen. It was Atari's most off-the-wall product. The men from Sears asked what they were smoking when they designed it, and one of the technicians stepped out from the back room and produced a lit joint.

On another occasion a dozen Sears people in three-piece suits came out to see Atari's new factory in Los Gatos. The people at Atari were wearing their usual T-shirts and jeans. Sensing the tension, Nolan placed giant empty cartons on the conveyor belt and, after everyone climbed into one, took the group on a tour of the factory. Later everyone went home, showered, and dressed for dinner. Hoping to make a better impression, the guys from Atari showed up in suits and ties, while the guys from Sears wore T-shirts and jeans.

*   *   *

Around the Valley, Nolan was known as King Pong. Atari was on a roll. If Atari was able to sell 150,000 Home Pongs exclusively through Sears in 1975, Nolan wondered how many more he could sell on the open market in 1976. To find out, he would first need to obtain the necessary capital. That was when Nolan paid a visit to Don Valentine, a local venture capitalist at Venture Capital Management Services in Menlo Park.

Venture capitalists invest in viable products, especially ones that, as the saying goes, cost a nickel to produce, sell for a dollar, and are habit-forming. Generally, venture capitalists like to put up between one hundred and six hundred thousand dollars in exchange for large chunks of stock, a seat on the board or some say in the company sometimes more than the founder himself, although this was not the case at Atari. Don Valentine engineered a venture capital syndicate with backers from around the country. Time Inc., and the Mayfield Fund, another California-based venture capitalist, matched the $600,000 Capital put into Atari; Fidelity Venture Associates of Boston kicked in another thirty thousand. With the $2.5–$3.5 million that Atari was earning, it was able to accumulate a capital base of nearly $4.5 million, which was worth a ten-million-dollar line of credit at the bank. But just as Pong was about to strike again, a new chip came along that revolutionized the video game industry.

6

IN EARLY 1976, General Instrument, a microelectronics company, introduced the AY38500, a single chip that provided game designers with four different paddle and two different shooting games. This economical six-in-one chip cost five to six dollars, depending on volume, dramatically reduced production costs, and made it possible to build a video game system for twenty-five to thirty-five dollars that would retail for sixty to seventy-five dollars. Suddenly, seventy companies, including RCA and National Semiconductor, were competing with Atari with basically the same games.

Initially, the chip was developed in 1975 by G.I. in Europe to be used in the production of European televisions. It was modified for American TV in 1976 in G.I.'s Long Island location. Due to the onslaught of video game manufacturers, which the chip helped create, G.I. was unable to meet a demand that was 50 to 60 percent higher than anyone had anticipated.

ZAP!

Coleco was the first to order the new superchip, which they received in time for Father's Day. By the end of 1976 Coleco sales were over $100 million. Lloyd's Electronics and many other small companies were less fortunate. They received only 20 percent of the chips they ordered. The company hardest hit was probably First Dimension of Nashville, which had purchased $1.5 million worth of suddenly outdated TTL circuitry parts right before the AY38500 came out.

In August the video game industry was turned around a second time when Fairchild Camera and Instruments debuted Channel F, the first full-color home video system to use replaceable cartridges. The game came with hockey and tennis built in. New game cartridges, including card, baseball, and tank war games, could be added as they were developed. Each cartridge contained a memory chip programmed with a specific game. The console used a newly developed Fairchild F8 microprocessor and four random-access memory chips. Channel F was competitively priced at $170. It made Atari's black and white dedicated game, which played only Pong, look as obsolete as a Brownie box camera compared to a Polaroid.

*   *   *

Nolan went for the whole enchilada and blew it. As usual, Nolan had spread himself too thin. People warned him not to go into two businesses at once. Most of Atari's capital was tied up in Pong games that wouldn't be sold until Christmas. In the coin-operated-game market, pinball was still king. Bally dominated the market. A successful pinball game had a production run of fifteen to twenty thousand units; the production run for the average video game was only three thousand. Although in 1976 Atari released Breakout and several successful driving games—LeMans, Night Driver, and Sprint 2—arcade space for video games was limited. It cost about a quarter of a million dollars to develop a game, and it was a proven fact that only one out of eleven video games earned substantial returns.

*   *   *

Grass Valley is a think tank in the Sierra that was started by two engineers, Larry Edmunds and Steve Meyer. Nolan knew Edmunds and Meyer from his Ampex days. Over the years he had asked their group to do more and more projects for Atari, until one day he announced he was buying them out. Grass Valley became Atari's Camp David, a retreat far away from the Valley where engineers could get stoned and dream up new ideas. Officially, this group of satellite engineers cut off from the mainstream of life was called Cyan Engineering, as in "cyan blue." Many of Atari's most important ideas came from here, including the X-Y monitor and the video computer system (VCS), Atari's first programmable home video game.

The VCS—Atari's little black control box—is actually a microcomputer. The game cartridge is the program, telling it what to do. Inside the box is a microprocessor. A microprocessor is an integrated circuit, but not all integrated circuits are microprocessors. A microprocessor is the room the size of a walk-in freezer inside the ENIAC computer shrunk down to the size of a chip. A microprocessor processes information very fast with the joy and inspiration of a postal clerk stamping and sorting envelopes, except the microprocessor does the job a million times faster and for a lot less money. It took a team of minds at Intel using the most sophisticated and highly specialized equipment thousands of man-hours and millions of dollars in research and development to create the microprocessor, most of which would end up in video games.

The VCS, code-named Stella, was conceived by Joe Decure, who designed the chip set and the first prototypes; Harold Lee, who had pushed Nolan in the direction of consumer electronics with Home Pong; and Steve Meyer, who figured out how to make the VCS cost-effective. The VCS was supposed to put Atari back in the home video ballgame, except Atari didn't have the money to perfect and manufacture it.

*   *   *

Just how thin did Nolan spread himself?

One day a twenty-year-old engineer named Steve Jobs showed up in Nolan's office. Jobs was an engineering student dropout who had a special deal with Nolan. Nolan would describe an arcade game and tell Jobs how many integrated circuits he wanted it to have. Jobs received a hundred-dollar bonus for every IC he saved. Jobs designed Breakout, the ultimate Pong game, in which every time the Pong ball hit a brick wall, it knocked out a brick until there were no bricks left. It was Pong turned inside out, and it was extremely successful. Breakout had thirty IC's, fifty fewer than specified; Jobs earned himself a five-thousand-dollar bonus.

Steve Jobs grew up in the Valley. He went to Homestead High. After school he sat in on lectures at Hewlett-Packard. One day, out of the blue, Jobs called up Bill Hewlett, president of the company and a perfect stranger and asked him if he could borrow some equipment for a machine he was building. Bill Hewlett said yes.

Jobs asked Nolan if he wanted to finance a minicomputer he and his buddy, Steve Wozniak, were building in Jobs's parents' garage in Los Altos. Until then they had been supporting their project by making and selling "blue boxes," illegal electronic telephone attachments that allow a caller to make free long-distance phone calls. Once "Woz" called up the Vatican, said he was Henry Kissinger, and asked to speak to the Pope. It was Woz, a college dropout who was designing calculators at Hewlett-Packard, who designed the prototype for an easy-to-use, desktop computer. He thought computer buffs would appreciate it. It was Jobs who saw the "personal" computer as a family item, something that could figure taxes, balance the checkbook, and do the kids' homework. Supposedly, Jobs badgered Woz into forming a company and commercializing his invention. They raised thirteen hundred dollars by selling Jobs's VW microbus and Woz's scientific calculator. When they went to the courthouse to make their company legal, they were told they needed a name for the company.

ZAP!

Jobs wanted a name that was homey and noncomputery, that wouldn't alienate the family. He came up with Apple.

Steve Jobs was recounting this story to Nolan, omitting, of course, that some of the parts for their computer may have been stolen from Atari. Their computer was based on the same principle as Atari's VCS, and Nolan should have jumped on it. Nolan's plate, however, was already full; he suggested that Jobs see Don Valentine, Atari's original investor. The last thing Nolan needed was to branch off into another business, the home computer.

Don Valentine went to check out the pint-size computer, with the prospect of investing a significant amount of cash into Apple in mind. To this very important meeting, Jobs wore cutoff jeans, sandals, shoulder-length hair and a Ho Chi Minh beard. Valentine took one look at Jobs and thought Nolan had to be kidding. But he did mention the home computer to Armas "Mike" Markkula, a former marketing manager at Intel who had retired in 1974 at the age of thirty-two, a millionaire. Markkula liked the computer so much, he put up $250,000 of his own money and came out of retirement to market the Apple. In return Jobs and Woz made him a full partner.

At first the company made 200 Apple I's, which they sold to retailers for the flip price of $666.66. Later they took the prototype, trimmed it down and polished it up, added a clear, easy-to-read instruction manual and sales skyrocketed from $2.7 million in 1977 to $200 million three years later. Although Jobs and Wozniak got all the credit, Valley insiders attribute much of Apple's success to Markkula's marketing genius.

*   *   *

Resigned to having passed up Jobs's personal computer project and to having to focus his attention on the wide-open home video game market, Nolan summoned Joe Keenan, Al Alcorn, Gene Lipkin, and the rest of the gang to his office. Nolan did not want what happened to coin-operated Pong—competitors with inferior games walking away with the lion's share of the profits—to happen to Home Pong. In order to seize command of the home video game market, Nolan desperately needed a large amount of quick cash to manufacture the VCS. He had two choices. Atari could go public, which, with the sagging economy and sinking stock prices, wasn't really a choice; or he could do the unthinkable and sell Atari. The gang drew up a shopping list of rich entertainment companies they thought had the proper "syzygy" to merge with Atari. MCA, which owned Universal Studios, and Disney were at the top of the list. Both passed. So did the other companies. Warner Communications wasn't even on the list.

NOLAN BUSHNELL: Everybody was losing interest in the digital watch and the pocket calculator, and most of the people we went to wondered why video games would be any different. Warner Communications was the only one with guts to put over $100 million into the company while everybody else was saying it was another CB radio.

ZAP!

*   *   *

Warner Communications is one of the biggest entertainment conglomerates in the world. Steve Ross, the high-rolling chairman of the board, is a lot like Nolan—or, rather, Nolan is a lot like Steve Ross, who is fifteen years older. Both are six-foot-five, energetic, charismatic, flamboyant risk-takers who surround themselves at the top with close friends. Both manage their companies in a laissez-faire style. Both are aggressive entrepreneurs who command respect and affection from the people they work with. Neither makes it as a day-to-day commanding officer. Both their companies had fantastic beginnings.

At age twenty, Ross, a poor Brooklyn Jew, married Carol Rosenthal. Her father owned Riverside Memorial Chapel and other funeral parlors in New York City. Every morning a hundred limousines left Ross's father-in-law's garage for funerals and returned in the evening. Ross was hanging out in the garage, noticed the idle limos, and was struck by an idea. He called up Carey Limousine Service and offered to rent them the hundred limos at ten dollars per night plus insurance and maintenance.

That idea brought three hundred thousand dollars a year in revenues into his father-in-law's fledgling limo rental business. A year later Ross was running a mediocre car rental business of his own when he made a deal with Kinney Systems, owner of the largest chain of parking lots in New York City. By increasing the number of car rental locations, Ross's business grew from 100 to 300 cars. The next year,

The Rise and Fall of Atari

1961, the two companies merged. After acquiring a cleaning business and a magazine and comic book distribution company, a mutual friend of Ross and Ted Ashley (owner of Ashley Famous, a Hollywood talent agency) insisted that they meet; by the end of the evening, Ross bought Ashley out and was in the entertainment business. From this Hollywood toehold, Ross bought Warner Bros.-Seven Arts in 1969 for about $400 million, which he paid for in Kinney stock. He could have chosen to go after ABC or MGM, though neither wanted to be acquired, but Warner's record division appealed to him more.

Along the way Ross divorced his first wife and married Amanda Burden—ex-wife of Carter Burden and daughter of Babe Paley; her stepfather is ex-CBS chairman Bill Paley. While vacationing in Disneyland with Amanda and his son from his first marriage, Ross went to make a phone call. When he returned, he found them totally absorbed in a video game eight people could play. The machine, he learned, was made by Atari; it sold for $4,500 and earned $250,000 a year. Around this time, Emanuel Gerard, one of four Warner executives who shared the newly created "office of the president," learned that Atari was for sale.

Atari made contact with Warner through Gordon Crawford, a capital research VP acquainted with Warner stock. Crawford approached Manny Gerard in the summer of 1976. Warner's biggest division, records and music publishing, had been red hot since the beginning of the early seventies, when pop music reached its pinnacle. Warner had superstar artists like Fleetwood Mac, Rod Stewart, Neil Young, Van

ZAP!

Morrison, Randy Newman, and the Beach Boys; but by the mid-seventies record sales took a dip. Suddenly Warner realized it wouldn't continue selling ten million Fleetwood Mac albums forever.

At the same time, production costs were up. Record companies pointed to the oil shortage—which in turn created a vinyl shortage—to explain why the retail price of records was so high. The real reason retail prices were up was that, after Fleetwood Mac's album *Rumors* was bought by 3 percent of the American population, Warner renegotiated with many of their major artists, giving them huge deals. In any event, rising prices certainly kept consumers away. And although Hollywood movies in general were enjoying a boom—about half of the top ten all-time movie grossers, including *Jaws* and *Godfather II*, were from that era—Warner's film division wasn't doing particularly well.

In 1976 people, especially kids, were ready for another form of entertainment. Music didn't have the meaning it had had in the late sixties and early seventies, when it was the main form of expression, and this left the door wide open for video games. Cash-rich Warner was desperate for a hot new product, and product-rich Atari was desperate for cash. The two companies were made for each other, except Warner never would have known it if it hadn't been for the tenacious Manny Gerard.

When Manny Gerard, a self-proclaimed loudmouth, joined Warner in 1974, he was reputed to be the best entertainment-industry analyst on Wall Street. Six months later Steve Ross made him executive vice president. Part of Gerard's job was to acquire properties. Atari was his first.

The Rise and Fall of Atari

It took four months to negotiate the deal. At one point, Nolan almost blew it when a local newspaper ran a photograph of Nolan and one of his girlfriends frolicking in a hot tub. Maybe his ex-wife, whom he'd recently divorced, saw it; maybe she read the article that parenthetically mentioned that Warner was buying Atari, because she turned up shortly thereafter and challenged Nolan's claim to his share in Atari. She was holding up the works, so Warner lawyers negotiated a settlement with her.

Nolan Bushnell can look you in the eye when he says he was twenty-nine years old when he started Atari with $250 of his own money and in four years had sold the company for $28 million, of which $15 million went into his pocket.

I T TOOK a lot of guts on Gerard's part to pull the deal off. It took a lot of vision to buy Atari. The company was nothing like it would become. It was a little one-sided—primarily an engineering company, which was all right, except that Warner had invested over $100 million in Atari. They were entering the consumer market with over 400,000 VCS's in November 1977, and they needed some merchandising. The profit margin for the VCS, which retailed for $200, wasn't that great, but the profit margin for the game cartridges, which retailed for twenty-five to thirty dollars and cost less than ten to produce, was awesome. Atari anticipated a tremendous Christmas rush, like the previous year, and so did everybody else.

In January 1977 RCA came out with Studio 2, a microprocessor-based, black and white video game system and a variety of game cartridges, of which bowling was probably the most popular. National Semiconductor, which had sold over 200,000 units of Adversary, which included built-in tennis and hockey, added soccer, pinball, and Wipe-out to their newer model. Fairchild, which had been back-ordered for the past six months, announced it would bring out a new cartridge every month. By the end of January, General Instrument had shipped seven million AY38500 chips and was preparing to introduce a new chip that pro-vided combat and racing games. Magnavox ordered the new G.I. chip for Odyssey 2, a new twenty-four-game, four-player video system it planned to sell for under a hundred dollars in September, while Allied Leisure was developing a backgammon game that was being touted as the next generation of electronic games. The whole video game in-dustry was awaiting the Christmas rush like a bunch of surfers paddling in the water waiting for the perfect wave.

The wave never came. Whether or not consumers were confused by the sheer number of different home video games, they didn't buy anybody's video product. Allied Lei-sure was the first to go under, before it could deliver. Na-tional Semiconductor was forced to stop production on its improved Adversary system. Magnavox canceled its twenty-four-game, four-player system. Fairchild and RCA dropped out of the video-game competition. Only Atari, buoyed by Warner money, and Coleco, which lost $30 million, survived the shakeout.

Manny Gerard's hands began to sweat. This was his first acquisition since coming to Warner, and here he was sitting on 400,000 VCS's. Nolan, who stayed on at Atari as chairman, supposedly running the company, spent more time up at his newly bought Folger mansion in Woodside than at the office. He wasn't returning Gerard's phone calls, which pissed Gerard off tremendously, nor was he taking calls from fuming shareholders.

"After we sold the company," said Joe Keenan, who remained as president of Atari and who was also made a multimillionaire by the Warner deal, "we didn't feel like busting our ass." Nolan shrugged, saying it wasn't as much fun playing with somebody else's money. Meanwhile Atari had $40 million tied up in inventory. Gerard started putting pressure on Nolan to find somebody who could manage the situation.

"They had no sales, no advertising or marketing, nothing but R&D," Manny complained.

Finally, Gerard sent in Ray Kassar, a no-nonsense former marketing VP from Burlington Industries, to straighten things out. Kassar knew nothing about computer games, but he knew something about corporate balance sheets.

Ray Kassar was the youngest vice president in Burlington's history. He left after twenty-five years, when he was passed over for the presidency, and started his own apparel company, making clothing in Egypt and selling it here. Atari was in the red when Gerard asked Kassar to go out to Sunnyvale, where Atari had moved its corporate headquarters in 1976, to see if he could turn the situation around. Kassar respected Gerard a lot, but said to himself, What do I need this for? After Burlington, Atari wasn't much of a company, and to Kassar, a sophisticated, cultured, society type used to hobnobbing in New York, Cairo, and other foreign capitals, Sunnyvale didn't sound too appealing. Gerard convinced him to fly out and take a look around. Ray shuttled back and forth a few times, consulting, but Gerard kept insisting that he stay permanently. Finally, Ray ran out of reasons to say no and took over the vacant office of president of the consumer division. First he stayed in hotels. Later, he moved into a very elaborate house in San Francisco and a rambling ranch-type house in Woodside. A limo took him to and from work.

Ray wore three-piece tailored suits, white shirts, and cufflinks. His tie had a perfect knot. He wore tinted glasses like Henry Kissinger. He didn't take a vacation for five years, worked weekends, and was at the office by 7:30 A.M., and didn't leave until after six. Nolan popped into the office, usually not until afternoon, dressed as if he had just stepped off the tennis court, which he usually had. Nolan believes that hard work doesn't necessarily lead to good results. Good results are a combination of work and fun. Kassar was a conservative, disciplined bottomliner, the exact opposite of Nolan, who was as impulsive as Francis Ford Coppola when it came to going over budget. One of them had to go.

* * *

The big blowout came in November 1978 at Warner's annual budget meeting in New York. Atari had grossed $120 million for the year, but sales didn't last past November. Atari still had a huge inventory. Warner brass wanted to know what Nolan was going to do in the coming year.

For the previous eight months Nolan had been dissatisfied with Atari's pinball project. He started the meeting by suggesting they shut that section of the company down because there was no innovation coming out of it. He warned them not to plan on launching a computer division unless they were prepared to put both feet in. He figured Atari would lose about $50 million just in establishing the new line; after that it would be profitable.

Nolan was building up a head of steam. When it came to VCS, he let it rip. The VCS retailed for two hundred dollars. If they dropped the price they could increase sales in the more profitable cartridges, Nolan shouted. If you cut the price of the VCS you will destroy the VCS's credibility, Manny screamed back. Looking back now, Nolan admits that Manny was probably right, but he's not sure Artari would have made any less money if they had gone his way. His numbers were calculated on the basis of three cartridges per VCS; Manny had figured seven per. For every additional VCS they sold, they would have made more on the profit margin than they had stuck in the VCS, and maybe they would have kept future competition out. The real issue was personalities. It was turning into an old-fashioned barroom brawl, right there in Warner's boardroom. In the end, Gerard yelled louder.

NOLAN BUSHNELL: Gerard and I got along famously at first. I still like Manny to this day, as an individual. But there's a difference between liking somebody and thinking he's a great businessman. In business we always had a problem, in approach and philosophy. We would have tremendous arguments but always with smiles on our faces. I told Manny

*to go to hell many times, but it didn't mean we didn't like
each other. Where we became unglued was when Manny
started killing the research projects. I saw that as building
a very fragile company. Manny wouldn't commit himself as
far as I thought he should. Manny is an entertainment analyst; he didn't fully grasp the diversity of engineering. He
thought a hundred million dollars in one project made a
lot more sense than a million dollars here and a million
dollars there. We were researching holography, everything.
We had a very powerful engineering team working on a lot
of projects—a lot more than Manny thought we should
have.*

The day after the meeting, over lunch, Nolan and Joe Keenan
reconsidered reorganizing the company as Gerard had pro-
posed several weeks earlier, with Nolan stepping down from
the chairmanship but staying on as director, Keenan moving up to the chairmanship, and Ray Kassar stepping in as
new chief executive. But when Nolan got back to California,
he began to have a change of heart. "I realized no matter
what the title was, the real shots were going to be called
from New York." Nolan decided he was just too rich to put
up with that. Meanwhile, Manny Gerard called an emergency
session of the board of directors, and Nolan was gone.
That's the version reported by the press.

*NOLAN BUSHNELL: When I got back to California I read
my contract. One clause stated that if I was fired I'd receive
$100,000 a year for four years, but if I quit I'd get nothing.*

ZAP!

That's why I wasn't showing up to work for a year and a half. I was forcing their hand. I had come to the conclusion that a company that, in my perception, was going to be screwed up long term was just something I didn't want to be associated with. I didn't see myself staying in a box. I always said I could make more money doing entrepreneurial things than working for somebody else. I called up Manny and told him I wasn't going to give up my position as CEO. I don't think there was any emergency meeting. I told him that he should exercise his right in the employment contract—I think it was Clause 1.1, which was their escape clause. Manny said "Okay," and fired me.

*   *   *

There's always a colonel. There's always a turning point. Someone decides he's had enough, puts his foot down, and there's a change. There are instances of this throughout history. A good example: The Civil War was dragging on in 1864. The South was almost winning. They had a smaller army, inferior logistics, but the Union couldn't finish them off. Lincoln's generals were making excuses for not attacking. Lincoln was a very practical man, and he knew these excuses weren't true. He heard about this guy named Grant who at the battles of Fredericksburg and Cold Harbor hadn't been afraid to lose 50,000 men. Lincoln said, "I want to see him."

Grant was a typical American. He'd failed in business in some little town in Ohio; he was alcoholic; his wife had left him; people thought he was washed up. But he sat down with Lincoln and said, "I know what to do." He wasn't afraid to lose 100,000 men, and he broke the stalemate at Vicksburg. There's always that turning point, that extra push that takes you over the top. And that's what happened at Atari.

Ray "the Czar" Kassar blew into Atari like a blast of Arctic air. He was like Grant at Vicksburg. He was detached and unemotional. Atari was in the red, and sales were loping slowly upward. To get Atari back in the black, he put it through a major contraction phase. He blew out superfluous operations, which in his terms meant R&D, and brought in salesmen and marketing people. Ray had come from a marketing background. He didn't fully understand why all this money was being spent developing products two or three years down the line when Atari couldn't get rid of products that had been gathering dust for the past two or three years. Maybe he should have added marketing to R&D rather than replace R&D with marketing. He reduced manpower, cut overhead, and generally streamlined the company. His major innovation was intensive advertising. That was Ray's big contribution, his supporters say.

Actually, the first thing Ray did as the new chief operating officer in early 1979, according to Valley gossip, was put a stop to the Friday afternoon "strategy sessions" that had been initiated by Nolan and were an Atari tradition. Then he put a freeze on R&D, meaning the development of future games. Bob Brown's team of thirty engineers was suddenly left with nothing to develop and was the first to go. Al Alcorn gave Bob the bad news. At first Bob didn't know what Al was talking about. "Kill R&D and you're killing the company's future." Gene Lipkin was out later that year when Ray pulled the plug on the pinball games his group was developing.

Other key engineers left for a combination of reasons. Most felt constrained by Warner's tight creative controls. Noah Anglin, VP of engineering at the time, had come over from IBM, where he had been labeled a wild duck who couldn't fly in formation. When Anglin came aboard Atari in 1976, a product took three months from conception to the time it got out the door. When he left in 1979, a product took a year or longer. Atari was turning into IBM, and he was still out of formation. Pretty soon everybody from the old days—two years before—was leaving. Some eventually came back to haunt Atari.

What happened at Atari is the classic story about growing businesses. There's an inflexion point in commercial growth. The entrepreneurs leave, and a new breed of people comes aboard. It's the same story you'll find in any business, but it happened faster and more dramatically at Atari.

8

ENGINEERS like Howard Delman and Harry Jenkins were fortunate to come early enough to observe both cultures. They were the first of the second generation of engineers at Atari. The first generation, guys like Al Alcorn and Steve Bristow, had built the video games Delman and Jenkins played while they were still in school. Even though they were fairly low in the ranks at the time, they still felt the repercussions going on in the company: Nolan being un- happy; Joe Keenan feeling uncomfortable; Lipkin being forced out. Alcorn stayed on longer than most of the early team, but he too was unhappy with the way the company was going.

Suddenly, free-spirited engineers needed magnetic ID cards to get from one corridor to another. Ray Kassar had put the lid on security. Even the names of the engineers were kept top secret. The official reason was to discourage jealousy among engineers, but it really was to prevent rival companies from stealing them. After Kassar arrived, it became easier to lay a sleeping bag down on the floor of the White House than for an unescorted visitor to walk into the employees' cafeteria at Atari and order a sandwich. In the Valley, in general, everything's nailed down. A video game takes twelve to fifteen months and costs from a quarter to three-quarters of a million dollars to develop, and a game is good for manufacturing for only two or three months. If somebody knew what Atari was up to and got a one-month jump on them, they could cut Atari's potential sales in half. And if somebody stole a game chip, which is cheap and easy to duplicate, it could save a rival millions of dollars in time and labor. On the average, there is about $20 million worth of theft reported in the Valley each year, one-third going to support the drug habits of speedfreaks and coke heads working on the assembly line. One day, to cut the boredom, a worker comes to work on speed, his production increases and he's put under pressure to keep up the same rate. That is why the former secret service man who was the agent in charge of protecting Presidents Nixon, Ford and Carter was made Director of Security at Atari.

Employees no longer showed up for work at their own pace; they had to be in by eight o'clock sharp. There were dress codes, time cards, and interoffice memos. Engineers who had been pampered under Nolan's regime were now regarded as spoiled brats. Kassar's total knowledge of electronics came out of the August 1979 issue of *Scientific American*, the one with the blow-up of a silicon chip on the cover, which Ray kept in the top drawer of his desk.

The Rise and Fall of Atari

HOWARD DELMAN: The essential difference between old Atari and new Atari is that all of the old management played games extensively, and none of the new management plays. It used to be that everybody played games. The secretary had access to games. I don't mean just video games—card games, chess, ball games, head games. Nolan, Joe, Al, and Gene loved games. When he put his mind to it, Nolan was usually the best. They'd get away from the boardroom and play. Now you won't find any game players above the level of programmers. Ray Kassar wouldn't be caught dead in an arcade.

The way Howard Delman came to Atari is corny. In 1976 he was doing graduate work at the University of California, Santa Barbara, and he was thinking about what to do after graduation. One day Howard was at Cold Springs in Santa Barbara, where he and his friends went to drink beer and play Tank, and he turned the game he was playing around to see who made it. That's when he decided to get a job at Atari. Video games were everything he was good at. He knew he could also design them.

He had grown up in Brooklyn, in back of his dad's TV repair shop. When he did graduate from UC, he got a job in Atari's coin-op division as a hardware engineer and programmer. He was twenty-four years old. There were about seven hundred people working at Atari in 1976, and very few were over thirty. Atari was still in Los Gatos, just before they moved corporate headquarters and engineering to Sunnyvale, and Nolan was still a prominent figure.

ZAP!

*   *   *

Harry Jenkins was doing graduate work at Stanford in 1976 when he met Nolan Bushnell for the first time in a restaurant. Nolan told Harry his name but Harry forgot it. He remembered Nolan's face though. Nolan was a tall, lanky guy with lots of charisma. He told Harry that he worked for this company that was really hip and that Harry should go down there and talk to them about a job when he got out of school. Everybody else told Harry to work at Hewlett-Packard, the great training ground for engineers. Harry did talk to H-P and to a few other companies that made high-technology products, and he decided they were all boring. Atari at least seemed interesting.

A year later, in 1977, Harry was sitting in the personnel office over at Atari, and this guy walked in wearing a Black Sabbath T-shirt and sneakers and invited him to the dedication of a new building. Harry asked the interviewer who that was, and she said it was Nolan Bushnell, the chairman of the board.

HARRY JENKINS: Al Alcorn was sitting up there on corporate row, and he really wanted to get out of that and back into day-to-day engineering. One day he ran into a guy with some holography who was coming down to Atari to give a presentation. I was basically kicking around the company, bootstrapping, when Al asked me if I wanted to come along. I thought the holography stuff was pretty neat, and I put together some concepts. Al took a look at them and said,

The Rise and Fall of Atari

"That's a product." I left the group I was with and went to work with Al.

They were chasing around Silicon Valley, looking for some space to build a lab. They walked into one building in an industrial park south of Sunnyvale, just off the Central Expressway, and Al started sniffing around with a funny look on his face. He walked outside, looked at the front of the building, and said, "This was Atari's first office building." It was where Al had built Pong.

* * *

While Alcorn and Jenkins spent most of 1978 developing their holographic product, carrying it all the way to soft-tooling, Howard Delman was working on Atari's first vector-generated hardware. Until then all video games, with the exception of Space Wars—the first vector-generated video game, which had been introduced a year earlier by an innovative San Diego-based company called Cinematronics—were based on raster scan, the process in which a lot of horizontal lines are drawn until they fill the entire picture tube; then an electron beam is turned on and off to excite the phosphor on the face of the tube. With vector scan, the electron beam moves from one point to another, rather than constantly scanning the entire screen. It's a line-drawing system, rather than a grid-drawing one, and it produces clearer, more realistic graphics.

In 1979, while Delman was programming Lunar Lander, Atari's first vector-generated game, Alcorn and Jenkins took a prototype of their holographic game to the trade show and wrote up orders that went way beyond the break-even point. Their product, however, was more of a hand-held electronic game, and Atari was a video game company.

Atari controlled three-quarters of the coin-operated video game market—no one controlled the home video game market as yet. Coin-op games were Atari's bread and butter. In order to build X number of Al and Harry's product, Atari would have to build half as many video games. Even though everybody thought it was a good product, Warner management said it was not the right time. That's when Al started to feel the time wasn't right for him to be at Atari.

*   *   *

While Alcorn was heading for the door, the totally unex-pected happened: The world discovered video games. Sales for 1979 were suddenly up 300 percent. It was all because of one game, Space Invaders, a fast-paced, action-packed, tension-mounting arcade shooting game in which the player blasted rows of crablike aliens as they relentlessly marched down the screen toward him. It was invented by the Taito Corporation, the Atari of Japan, and was licensed here by Atari's arch rival, Bally's Midway.

Until Space Invaders, Midway had commanded about a fifth of the arcade video game market. When Taito first introduced the game in Japan a year earlier, the reaction was so phenomenal it caused a coin shortage. The Japa-nese government had to quadruple the yen supply, just so kids could feed the machines. The reaction to Space Invaders here was similar to what had happened when Pong showed up for the first time at Andy Capp's, except on a much grander scale.

Whenever something great comes along in a given field, like Mohammad Ali in boxing, suddenly there's a surge of interest in that field. Space Invaders unquestionably is the Mohammad Ali of video games, the one that got the press, TV, and everyone playing video games.

Before the 1970s, the video game, as a commercial concept, didn't exist. Then, when it did, it wasn't conceived of on its own terms—just as when stainless steel was first used as a building material, especially in elevators, it was made to look not like steel but like wood. The first video games used the newest technology to play a very old game, Ping-Pong, and its variations, tennis and hockey, before moving on to driving games and then traditional games like baseball and football.

But it wasn't until Space Invaders that video games began to utilize the full potential of the technology that went into creating them. Pong wasn't as exciting as Ping-Pong, but Space Invaders was more exciting than bowling, which is very much what Space Invaders was like, except Space Invaders was about twenty times faster. Space Invaders was much faster than its predecessors, with more audio and action. With Space Invaders, video games evolved from a friendly game of Ping-Pong into a violent life-and-death struggle. This was when kids started blowing their allowances and lunch money in the arcades; when they started missing classes, skipping their homework, and learning to kill things dispassionately. Kids stopped listening to music, reading books, and playing sports. Space Invaders was a new form of entertainment that appealed to kids who had not been exposed to the old forms of entertainment.

Taito might not admit it, but Space Invaders was really a reverse form of Atari's Breakout, the most popular video arcade game preceding Space Invaders. Atari once attempted a reversal of Breakout, which wasn't too successful, called Avalanche, in which puff balls and rocks fell from the top of the screen while the player had to catch them with several paddles that moved back and forth across the bottom. As the game progressed, the rocks and puff balls grew smaller and fell faster, and there were fewer and fewer paddles with which to catch them. It could actually be said that Space Invaders put faces on those rocks, and instead of catching them, the player had to shoot them.

By the end of 1979 Space Invaders had sold a record-breaking 350,000 units worldwide; 55,000 of them in America. More importantly, it also created a craze in home video games. Atari VCS sales went through the roof. Atari unloaded their entire inventory of 400,000 units so fast, that Atari had to ration them. Ray Kassar came out looking like a hero. According to Warner, Ray turned the home video game from a Christmas product into a year-round item. Some credit should go to Nolan, however, who was just as much responsible for building up that inventory as Kassar.

NOLAN BUSHNELL: During my final year at Atari, the company did an analysis of what the public would buy. The

The Rise and Fall of Atari

VCS's production figures were based on that, but the stores wouldn't believe them and consequently were under-stocked. The VCS sold out at the big department stores back East by December 16, when it was too late to reorder for the Christmas rush. That stuff didn't sit around for two years as Warner claims. Look at the sales figures the year I left, 1978, and figure out how much a VCS sells for and when they would have sold out. Don't forget, I also hired Ray. If there was a problem in marketing, as Warner claims, I solved that problem by hiring Ray.

Ray was an enormously sophisticated man. He went to the ballet to see Baryshnikov; he did not play Space Invaders. It was his idea, however, to license Space Invaders for Atari's VCS. It was the first time a company licensed an arcade game for a home video system. The cartridge was pro-grammed by a bizarre fellow who left the company about six months later, suffering, from "programmer burnout." Atari's Space Invaders was released amid a great deal of fanfare and, like the coin-operated game, took the world by storm. Revenues for 1980 doubled to about $415 million, and operating income quintupled to $77 million, one-third of Warner's total 1980 operating income. In six months Warner stock shot up 35 percent. Atari was the fastest grow-ing company in the history of America. Ray himself an-nounced that at one of Atari's dinners.

Atari could have designed original home video games, like, say, Bocciball, and put them on the shelf next to Missile Command, a highly successful coin-op game, but everybody bought titles they recognized, the ones they played in arcades. Bocciball may have been a better game, but sales for a recognizable title were three to five times better than for any original cartridge. Therefore, Atari went license-crazy.

Atari licensed Space Invaders, its first million-selling cartridge, with the money it made from an arcade game called Asteroids, Atari's answer to Midway, released in November 1979. Asteroids sold 70,000 units, at $2,700 a shot, by the end of 1980 and replaced Space Invaders as the all-time best-selling video game. Asteroids, in fact, was the first game in Atari history that workers stopped the production line in order to play.

9

"THERE was a game called Asteroids, the most successful computer game of all up until that time, in the lab when I left Atari," said Nolan. "And some modifications were made after I left, so it's hard to say who gets credit for authorship."

"The original game idea for Asteroids is mine," said Lyle Rains. "However, I didn't work on the technical team that did the game. That was done by a group of engineers because basically I was a manager by then. The actual credit goes to the engineers who worked on the game."

Twenty-nine-year-old Lyle Rains graduated from Berkeley in 1973 and came directly to the coin-op division at Atari, after arcade Pong and before the home version. He thought he'd work for about a year and then go back to school. The first game he worked on was Tank, a game Steve Bristow had conceived, in which two little bug-shaped

tanks shot at each other on a field with mines in the center.
Then came Jet Fighter, Steeple Chase, Spring II, and Canyon Bomber.

Lyle never went back to school. There was Cosmos,
a two-man, tabletop game with a holographic display including a few planets and some asteroids, which Harry and
Al had worked on. The asteroids didn't move, but while you
were flying around fighting it out with the other player's
spacecraft, you could shoot them if you wanted. There were
so many demands on Atari's production capabilities at the
time that the game never left the lab on the ground floor
of the engineering building. The game never left Lyle's mind,
either. He'd think about it while driving home from work,
while getting something to eat, in the shower—especially
around the time Space Invaders came out. Somewhere
along the line it suddenly occurred to him: What if those
rocks moved around?

Lyle mentioned the idea to Delman, who thought he
had some hardware to put the idea up on, and to Ed Logg,
a thirty-two-year-old programmer who had worked at Control Data for five years before coming to Atari. Before Asteroids, Logg had worked on Dirtbike, Super Breakout, Video
Pinball, and Football. Two weeks after Lyle mentioned the
project to him, Logg had a working prototype. Pretty soon
all his buddies were dropping into his lab, and he couldn't
get them to leave. He ended up building two prototypes,
one for him to work on and the other for his buddies to
play.

The "Fifth Beatle" on the Asteroids design team was

The Rise and Fall of Atari

Don Osborne, vice president of sales and marketing at Atari's coin-op division. He doesn't get the credit, but he was as much responsible for the game's success as any of the design engineers.

Because Atari was now basically a marketing company, Don Osborne was in a heavier position than, say, a vice president of engineering. Whatever engineering came up with, it was Don Osborne's department that had to sell it. He was neither old Atari nor new Atari. He was transitional Atari, having arrived about the time Ray Kassar did. Everyone laughed at him when he showed up to work his first day in a three-piece suit. Now it wasn't funny anymore. Everyone at Atari wore three-piece suits.

DON OSBORNE: I came to Atari in late '76, when Atari was trying to get into the pinball business. We did get in, unfortunately. At that particular point in time in the coin-machine business, pinball was king. Distributors and operators around the country were making their money with pinball. They were still making a lot of money on pool tables and a fair amount of money with jukeboxes, but pinball was the dominant force in the street locations. As opposed to the arcade locations, the street locations really constitute a much larger segment of the business. When you had a successful pinball game, you produced fifteen to twenty thousand units. On the other side of the coin, the average video game made maybe a three-thousand- or two-thousand-unit run.

So Atari aimed to be in the pinball business, but it also

wanted to bring something new to it. Atari's first and only effort was in solid state. We were the first to expand the playing field. We had the most expensive pinball game on the market at the time. It was $1,295 to the distributor, which was an awful lot of money then. That was the Atarian.

The early experiences with pinball were actually very exciting. The manufacturing wasn't. It was very difficult to produce a pinball game in this Valley, because the suppliers were in Chicago. Our games were not very reliable. But it was just the beginning. We made five more, including Hercules, the largest pinball ever made; Middle Earth, the first game with two playing fields; Superman, which was incredibly successful, but we could only go thirty-five thousand units because we couldn't produce them fast enough. Bally could have produced in two weeks what took us four months, which is why we dropped out of pinball in 1979.

In '78, Space Invaders had come on. Although Space Invaders was fantastically successful, everybody thought it was a one-shot fluke. We had launched Football at the same time as Space Invaders and that was a very successful game for us, but it tended to be kind of seasonal, as football is. Football earned about as much as Space Invaders for the first 90 to 120 days, but Space Invaders kept going after Football died off. Then came Asteroids; Asteroids surpassed Space Invaders. That's when the business community started to think that maybe video games weren't flukes. As video progressed, everything that competed with it was left in its wake. The operator, no matter what amount of money he had to invest in coin machines, would pour it into videos.

The Rise and Fall of Atari

When Osborne marketed Asteroids, he did something he had never done before. He got into his car one Friday night and drove to a location they had up in Sacramento and watched an interesting occurrence. People went from Space Invaders to Asteroids, back to Space Invaders and returned to Asteroids. The games were very different, but the players were related. Osborne figured if Asteroids got half the business Space Invaders got, Atari would also make a lot of money.

DON OSBORNE: We took Asteroids to the national trade show in Chicago in November 1979, but the game was not well received. They did not recognize Space Invaders either for the success it became. They did not recognize Tank, did not recognize Pong. We didn't even take orders on Asteroids. Instead we told the operators and distributors, "Take these samples and at the end of two weeks, if you feel the way we do, we'd like to see a bigger order." Of course it exceeded everybody's expectations. We were hoping Asteroids would get us through June 1980. Production of coin-op Asteroids lasted until March 1981.

Before Space Invaders, the difference between coin-operated and home video games didn't matter, because the Pong-type games that existed were simple and the market was relatively very small. By Space Invaders, home video technology and the home video market had been developed to a point where the differences did matter.

The first difference is that the monitor in home video

is the player's television set, and that puts certain limits on the resolution of the video image that can be presented. The picture on a coin-op game can be at least twice as complex as that on the home video.

The second major difference is that home video games generally work with a fixed system because they are mass produced, whereas coin-op games, which are produced in comparatively smaller lots, are free to develop new systems to do special things, which has allowed designers to come up with a totally different display technology, such as the vector display system.

Asteroids is an example. There is a game processor and a display processor. The game processor controls everything that goes on in the game—how and where the ships go, how and where the rocks go, when there will be collisions, the scoring, and the audios. The game processor tells the display processor to put the rocketships and rocks up on the display and actually creates the visuals. The third major difference is that coin-op games have a lot more in terms of electronics and special effects than the consumer-type models. Therefore, coin-op games tend to be a little flashier, a little more advanced and complex, and one, two, or three years ahead of what will be available for the home.

10

THE FIRST pop stars were movie stars, followed by rock stars and jocks. Then Space Invaders and Asteroids came along. People didn't see as many movies, buy as many records, or see as many sporting events. They played video games instead. Designers, the glorified term for programmers, became the new culture heroes. Instead of going to Hollywood to write the Great American Screenplay, bright technobrats were coming to the Valley to write the Great American Video-Game Program. Instead of typing words on a typewriter, this new breed of writer pounded a keyboard that produced images on a screen. It is a lot easier to produce a video game than it is to raise millions of dollars to produce a movie. For a few hundred dollars a person could go out and buy a computer and do everything himself from his chair.

A programmer is easy to spot at Atari. He's not wearing

a suit and tie. He's wearing jeans, a T-shirt, and Hushpuppies. He has sideburns and long hair. Fashionwise he is still in the sixties. He and most of his colleagues, with the exception of Donna Bailey who programmed Centipede and is one of a handful of women programmers in the entire industry, are men in their mid-twenties. Before he quit school he was regarded as a nerd. He didn't play ball, didn't date girls, couldn't dance. He was into only one thing, computers—and that turned out to be the biggest thing happening. Now he gets the best girls, people look up to him, he's a superstar.

Not all programmers are engineers. Some were music students who learned to program, or engineering students who took some art courses. Others never finished school. Atari hired them because they seemed to understand what made a game sell. Atari figured there were at least a million people out there who could write a program, a hundred who could write an interesting program, and maybe ten who could write a blockbuster. There are too few great video designers to say what it takes to be one. It seems to be a combination of technical skill, artistry, and magic.

It's just as difficult to say what constitutes a good game, hit song, or movie. If there were a formula to follow, there would be no flops. According to experts, Space Invaders was a fluke. Asteroids was too simple. They thought shooting games would be the only successful games. Then Pac-Man, a maze game, came along. Experts said Pac-Man was too dumb. The same was said about Donkey Kong, a climbing game; Dungeons and Dragons, an adventure game;

and Dig Dug, a strategy game. Of course, these games were megahits.

The true battle in the arcade is not between the player and the computer, but the player and the arcade operator. Although the machine always wins, the longer it takes, the fewer quarters will be in the cashbox. The experienced player reads a screen the way a trout fisherman reads a stream. The skills involved in a game seem unattainable at first, but the player knows the screen is two-dimensional; he can move either horizontally or vertically. At some point there will be holographic games, where the player will be able to move forward and backward. The first few times, even the best of players are wiped out immediately. The adept player quickly learns to correct his mistakes. Players who excel at Gravitar, a shooting game, are those who played Lunar Lander successfully, then Asteroids, then Defender, picking up a set of skills along the way. Some players are inclined to strategy games or maze-type games like Pac-Man and Berserk; others prefer rescue-type games like Donkey Kong and Kangaroo. The more he plays, the quicker the player develops a game plan that works. By following certain successful patterns over and over, Pac-Maniacs were able to stretch their quarters, but for every player who mastered Pac-Man, a far greater number played the game for the first time. Pac-Man is the most successful video game to date. Operators complained that the players weren't stuffing quarters into the machines fast enough, so the designer made the newer units with a faster Pac-Man and altered the patterns.

ZAP!

Usually, coin-op video games that earn well in one location earn well in all locations. There were exceptions. Breakout was big in Florida, Philadelphia, and Wisconsin but not in Los Angeles or Portland. The criterion for good coin-op games is generally the same all over: They must be easy to learn but difficult to master. If a game is too easy, the player masters it after a few quarters. If it's too difficult, he stops playing after a few quarters. The trick in coin-operated games is to make the player want to put another coin in.

Game cartridges tend to be equally popular throughout the country, except for pockets here and there where games seem to thrive more than in other regions. For some reason, checkers-type games do better in farming areas in the Midwest. Chicago is a backgammon town; Oklahoma City isn't. The appeal of Defender, Berserk, and Pac-Man is universal.

Cartridges tend to fall into various gaming categories: sports, skill, strategy, adventure, and space games. In addition, games are either original or adapted from popular arcade games. Home video games do not face the same problem that arcade games do. Games at home can take hours to play. It is not economical to do that with a coin-operated game. In the highest level of a chess cartridge, the player can wait ten hours for the computer to make its move. The player flips the TV off, and leaves the game plugged in. In the morning, he turns the TV back on to see what the computer did.

*   *   *

The Rise and Fall of Atari

A programmer at Atari, whether in coin-op, in consumer electronics, or off in some R&D group, functions somewhat the same. Inside his head is an unlimited number of game ideas. Outside are unlimited amounts of cash. What happens in each division typically depends on which idea the programmer can convince someone in management to let him work on. His development station, which is in a windowless room shared with six or so other engineers, at similar stations, consists of a black box, which is a VCS with a bunch of RAM's inside instead of a cartridge; an ordinary Sony TV and a logic analyzer, which is to the video programmer what a stethoscope is to a doctor. He sits at a keyboard and starts putting lines up on the screen. It may take him two or three months to get the full picture. He is a software engineer, technically, and a clever guy. He doesn't have to know how to draw. If he needs a spaceship, he draws some dumb spaceship. A graphic artist will improve it later. The trick is to make an entertaining game to fit the amount of space the consumer can afford. The real work is getting the picture up on the screen in the first place. Once he does that, the logic tells the objects to move around so that this missile hits that ship. If he blows up a ship, he gets points.

When he has the game 70 percent completed, he shows the prototype to a focus group of between twenty and forty people, which is divided according to age: sixteen- to eighteen-year-olds and nineteen- to thirty-five-year-olds. These people are recruited from Atari's warranty cards. There's nothing they'd rather do than be paid twenty dollars to play video games for two hours.

First they are screened to make sure they play three to five times a week. The designer sits behind one-way mirrors watching them react to his game; a facilitator asks them questions about what they like and dislike about the game play, the sounds, the graphics. The designer sits behind the mirrors with a tape recorder while these clowns criticize his beautiful game. The idea of a focus group is to give feedback on ways to improve the game or problems they had playing it. The designer takes this information back to the lab and cries. Then he refines his game design. When the game's buttoned up, it goes to play testing. There the game is played by 100 to 110 people, a cross section of light, medium, and heavy users. Men, women, and kids. They're called the General Public. The designer's no longer looking for feedback and improvements. This is the moment of truth: He's looking for a Nielson rating.

When a game designer in coin-op receives approval to develop an arcade game, the engineering department builds a breadboard of it. A breadboard consists of many integrated circuits, vermicelli wiring, a power supply in back, and a computer terminal so the designer can communicate with the system. The advantage of a breadboard, from an engineering point of view, is that you can change the parts around until the whole thing behaves the way you want it to. The only problem is you can't sell a thing like a breadboard to the public. It's too ugly, too big, and uses too much juice. All this stuff has to be shrunk down to the size of a few chips.

Although this department is called LSI design, very

large-scale integrated circuits (VLSI) are designed here. What they produce is a map, not an actual integrated circuit, of what looks like all the streets and turns found on the VLSI, which is encoded by numbers on a piece of magnetic computer tape so the map can be reproduced someplace else. The tape is sent to a semiconductor supplier. From these tapes the supplier can generate plates that represent the functions of the breadboard. Ultimately, this information is squeezed onto a chip. The semiconductor supplier doesn't work for Atari exclusively, and before he is given the tape he has to sign a lot of agreements about confidentiality.

The entire process of making a video game at Atari, from the moment of conception to the moment it reaches the arcade, if it's a coin-operated game, or a store's shelf, if it's a cartridge game, takes anywhere from nine to fifteen months, in which time the designer may have worked on two or three new games, or he may have left Atari and gone out on his own.

*   *   *

Just as the three giant chip-makers, Advanced Micro Devices, Intel, and National Semiconductor, were started by rebellious engineers from Fairchild, so a number of video game companies were spawned by Atari, beginning in 1979 with Activision. Alan Miller, David Crane, Bob Whitehead, and Larry Kaplan, four highly respected but totally disenchanted software engineers from Atari, had the idea of forming their own company that would design video games to be played on the Atari VCS.

At the time, two-thirds of the game consoles in homes across America were VCS's, and the average owner was buying at least five game cartridges a year. They ran into Jim Leavy, a marketing VP at GRT, a defunct record and tape outfit in Sunnyvale, who was about to buy out the livelier fledgling divisions. He knew nothing about video games, but he knew about stereos and how the industry had developed over the past thirty years.

Both the VCS and the record player—the hardware—cost more money to produce and yielded less profit than the cartridges and records—the software—they played. The most sophisticated video game cost about five dollars to produce and earned three times that in profit. Jim Leavy went back to his venture capitalist and told him that instead of acquiring a business, he was going to start one. He received $700,000, twice the amount he had originally asked for.

No one had the guts to make software compatible with someone else's hardware until Activision came out of nowhere and challenged mighty Warner Communications with graphically superior games like Tennis, Hockey, Freeway, and Kaboom. Their first year in business, 1980, Activision sold $65.9 million in software, for a profit of $12.9 million. At first their success had no adverse effect on Atari. People actually went out and bought the VCS so they could play Activision's games. Ten of Activision's first sixteen games marketed in 1980 were designed by Miller and Crane, Activision's most publicized designers. Neither had planned on becoming a designer.

The Rise and Fall of Atari

After graduating from the University of Berkeley where he majored in electrical engineering, specializing in large-scale computer system analysis, Miller took a straight job with a company that built control systems for lumber mills. This was back when Nolan Bushnell was putting the finishing touches on Pong. Miller, in fact, played Pong at Andy Capp's, his favorite hangout, when it was first tested there. He spent the next two years at NASA and a semiconductor company before answering an Atari ad in the help-wanted section of a local newspaper in 1977.

Atari was about to come out with its VCS and needed engineers who could design game cartridges. Miller's first project was to convert Surround, a fairly popular arcade game, into the home video version. He went out to the arcades, which he had never done before, and played the game until he saw which improvements to make. He also designed Hangman and Basketball and contributed to Atari's two home computers, the 800 and 400, before leaving the company two and a half years later.

David Crane, twenty-eight, had been into consumer electronics since he started playing pinball before he was ten years old. He still plays every arcade game that comes out. After graduating from the DeVry School of Technology in Phoenix, he worked at National Semiconductor for two years. He met Alan Miller at an apartment complex in Sunnyvale where they both lived, and Al recruited him to work with him at the programming department of Atari. He also worked on the 800 and 400 home computers before going to Activision.

ZAP!

Impressed with Activision's rapid success, William F. X. Grubb, a former vice president of marketing at Atari, started Imagic, the second Atari spinoff, in September 1981 with a staff of Atari and Activision defectors. A software-only company like Activision, Imagic added a new wrinkle by designing games for Atari's VCS and Mattel's Intellivision when it entered the market. Imagic shipped its first game in March 1982 and by June was doing $15 million in business. Rob Fulop, twenty-four, an ex-Atari engineer seeking fame and fortune, joined Imagic in the middle of that year and became the company's first superstar designer. His first project, Demon Attack, shipped $30 million in sales by the end of the year.

*   *   *

Before he left the company, Howie Delman epitomized the Atari video-game designer. He looked more like a rock star, like Billy Joel in fact, than an electrical engineer. (Of course, there are those who would argue that Billy Joel looks more like an electrical engineer than a rock star.) Delman is one of those ten in a million programmers Atari considered very special. Most hardware designers—engineers who physically build the game—know something about programming but don't qualify as programmers. Likewise, most programmers know something about hardware design but don't qualify as hardware designers. Delman qualifies as both.

In addition to designing and programming Lunar Lander (Atari's first vector, or x-y game), he also built Asteroids

96

and Battlezone, three of Atari's most popular arcade games up to that point. He programmed Fire Truck and Smokey Joe and did both the programming and hardware for two other Atari arcade hits, Superbug and Canyon Bomber. Not only did Delman build Asteroids' complicated circuitry, he was responsible for the game's eleven distinctive sounds. His musical background consisted of listening to records of mostly older rock bands like the Who, the Moody Blues, Buffalo Springfield, and early Elton John. He was working on a game he'd conceived, designed the hardware for, and was in the middle of programming when he quit Atari in 1981 because Atari had stopped being fun.

HOWARD DELMAN: When I first came to Atari, all of us in the department were friends. It was like a family. We all socialized. We did everything together. We could talk about the past. Then the engineering department, particularly electrical, doubled in size from forty to eighty people in eighteen months. When you grow that fast, people don't have time to become part of the group. I think it grew too fast. Productivity went down because people were busy training other people. When I started there I was in awe of the people. They were without doubt the most brilliant minds put in one place. As the company kept growing, the standards went way down. I found myself unable to pursue the things I was interested in. I became, by nobody's fault, a supervisor, which was something I aggressively pursued. At the time I took the job, it was relatively easy and didn't take a lot of my time. As the department grew, so did the job of supervisor. I spent less time doing what I enjoyed. As the company grew, it became more structured. Things weren't done just off the cuff. There was planning, meetings, etc. The company focused on what it saw as its market and what a good product was. It got a little frustrating to roll up my sleeves, dive in, and come up empty-handed. Two other engineers, Roger Hector and Ed Rotberg, and myself all shared the same sympathies. We wanted to make all the money ourselves.

Ray called Delman into his office and asked him why he was quitting. Delman told him. Ray asked if everybody felt the same way, and Delman told him if they didn't they ought to. Collectively the three engineers had created over a dozen successful Atari arcade games and some blockbusters. According to Delman, Ray hated to see the three go.

Ray had dealt with irate engineers before but understood very little about them. Engineering was the furthest thing from his background. "We treat them like we treat any other superstars," Ray told a leading business magazine, referring to the engineers as "high-strung prima donnas." Shortly thereafter a lot of the engineers, led by Delman, sported T-shirts that said, "I'm just another high-strung prima donna superstar."

HOWARD DELMAN: Programmers at Atari had super rock star images. You can compare the game industry today with the film industry of the thirties. All the stars were owned by the studios; they had no choice as to what films they'd make. Eventually in the forties and fifties the stars realized that it was a two-way street. They split from the studios, got agents, and worked on a film-by-film basis for whomever. We're seeing that now with programmers. There are programmers' agents out there. As the eighties go on you'll see more and more creative people selling their services.

Ed Rotberg knew the end was near when facilities, Atari's maintenance division, took over the best parking spaces. He had come to Atari in 1979 after seeing an Atari ad in *Computer World* for a microcomputer programmer. He joined the software engineering department while Asteroids was going strong. Atari was still a fun place to work. One of Rotberg's projects was Atari Baseball. His last was Battlezone, which he worked on with Howard Delman and Roger Hector. Battlezone, a tank-versus-tank game fought on a three-dimensional landscape, was the most innovative game of its time. It was Atari's first first-person game. The player did the shooting, not a third party like the laser cannons in Space Invaders or the space ship in Asteroids.

In Battlezone, the players looked through a periscope at a bird's eye view of the action. It took three microprocessors, some tricky engineering by Delman, and Roger Hector's realistic graphics to achieve this effect. Rotberg did the programming. Atari sold 75,000 units at $3,000 each. The U.S. Army was so impressed they ordered their own specially modified version to train troops on. Rotberg got into a big fight with management at one of the early planning sessions. He argued that Atari shouldn't work for the

ZAP!

government. He spent two months working on the trainer,
hating every minute of it. He figured he'd rather work for
himself.

*ED ROTBERG: Before leaving, Howie and I went out and
painted the reserved parking sign over. It turns out after we
left, Maintenance sprayed it back. Since we left, nobody had
the nerve to paint it out again.*

Of the three superstar engineers, Roger Hector looked the
least like a rock star. He wore suits and ties and was more
laidback. Now in his early thirties, he joined Atari in 1976
as a concept and video graphic designer, specializing in the
important field of holographic display, and rose to corporate
manager of advanced projects, a corporate R&D group, in
1980. He reported directly to the chairman. Roger's problem
was that Kassar didn't know what he was talking about.

*ROGER HECTOR: Ray just never said no. He went on faith.
The types of things I really wanted and couldn't get were
production commitments for some of the products we fully
developed. That is the point where all the yesses turned to
noes.*

HOWARD DELMAN: Did you ever ask for a car?

*ROGER HECTOR: You know, I never did. I'm sure I could
have got it. Before I left Atari there was a company called*

100

The Rise and Fall of Atari

Holosonics whose sole purpose was to assemble, under one roof, all the significant patents surrounding the field of holography. They were trying to be a clearinghouse for all of holography, but once they acquired all these patents they didn't do anything with them. They went belly up. Holosonics' patent package, which amounted to about 90 percent of everything that was ever done, sat in receivership with a bank up in Oregon, where it languished for sale for a long time. Anyone could buy, but the trouble was the bank had no idea what it had. They thought it was worth a load of money. The fact that nobody ever tried to buy it for years never fazed them. What they failed to realize was that a patent has a lifespan and is worth a lot less the further into the patent you get. There were a few years left, but it was getting to the critical point where you could sell any of it. Nonetheless, Atari stepped up and bought it.

Ironically, after Al Alcorn quit, Roger was the only actively involved one in the company with holographic know-how. Insiders said they will be surprised if Atari does anything with it.

While other former Atari engineers went on to develop software-only companies that could be played on Atari hardware, Delman, Hector, and Rotberg concentrated on a business of their own making, expanding the hardware base of the coin-op game to new levels of technology, such as holographic and three-dimensional display. In the spirit of Valley entrepreneurialism, they put their careers, security, and savings on the line and founded Videa, an electronic

ZAP!

entertainment company—not strictly a video game company. Originally their idea was to license their products to someone else to manufacture. Conceivably they could have licensed a game to Atari, but they wanted to establish their independence first. If they began designing for Atari right off the bat, they might always be viewed as an Atari company, which they wanted to make clear they were not. Instead, they were viewed—at least by Atari—as Nolan's "three stooges," since they rented space in a building he owned and shared his philosophy.

11

AN ORIGINAL Computer Space stands like a shrine outside Steve Bristow's office at 1349 Moffett Park Drive in Sunnyvale. It's the oldest artifact at Atari and maybe in the entire Valley, where anything not state-of-the-art is ancient. Around here, thirty-two-year-old Steve Bristow is considered a dinosaur. Officially, he's the oldest ranking employee at Atari. "Actually, the oldest ranking employee is Cynthia," he says, "who used to babysit for Nolan's daughters." The summer she graduated from high school she needed a job, so Nolan hired her as his secretary. Steve was doing part-time wire-wrapping in the building but wasn't on the payroll. Now Cynthia is in the computer group as a program tester.

Bristow looks more like a folksinger than vice president of engineering. Through the years he has seen Nolan, Joe Keenan, Al Alcorn, Gene Lipkin, and his other friends leave. Some went on to other companies and became very successful. Certainly the opportunity to leave has presented itself many times.

STEVE BRISTOW: I had been treated fairly well, and the opportunity still exists to develop new products. I wasn't looking forward to the sale particularly, because I didn't come out as well as Nolan, but I was at least going to have security as far as financing was concerned. I've seen a lot of companies get bought out around here, but if I could pick out who I'd like to be bought out by, Warner would be my choice. They're willing to put their balls on the line, which is more than a G.E. or a transformer company from the Midwest could say.

Bristow runs an R&D group of about thirty engineers, which functions as a little side company working on new products like the 5200 Super VCS and Ataritel, a computerized system that hooks up to the telephone the way the video game computer hooks up to the television. Bristow has a refrigerator in the back room, full of beer that is broken out on Fridays. Steve still finds attributes of the old Atari, but the company's obviously bigger now and has some uptight attributes of General Motors, too.

Harry Jenkins expected to come to Atari in 1977, work two or three years and then go out and start his own company.

HARRY JENKINS: Probably one of the easiest things in the world to do is to leave Atari, get venture capital, and start another company. The only way to keep people around is to take care of them. You can't throw enough money to keep them here if they're not happy.

Atari had set up a number of plush garages around the company for some of their engineers to tinker in, and Jenkins has been in one of them since he worked with Al Alcorn. His job at Atari is the only job he's ever had. His whole work experience since coming out of school has meant a good salary, open budget, and no bosses.

HARRY JENKINS: There is still a sense of entrepreneurialism alive in the company, and it primarily exists in R&D groups, which are like technological guerillas spread around the company. These groups are autonomous. Anything you want you can get. It's like running your own company. Warner movies are organized the same way, with lab companies and Orion Pictures. The entertainment industry is predicated on rapidly changing technology and short product life cycles. The fact that we have all these independents out here running it is really going to be the future of the company. I oversee this group, and other guys oversee other ones. I have a boss I report to named Alan Kay. I used to report directly to Ray Kassar, but he hired a chief scientist, and it made no sense for me to report to Ray. He did not know what we were working on on a day-to-day basis. I'm an engineer. He's a merchant. He's very, very good at that. When I came here we had products sitting in the warehouse. Great products, and we've made a lot of money off them since, and Ray's genius was in setting up a real advertising and marketing organization. He's got a real good nose for what's going to sell. He may not understand ROMs and RAMs, but boy he's got a real sense of what's going to sell.

There are different forms of R&D at Atari. One form is exile. R&D is Atari's Siberia. (There are certain engineers at Atari who don't fit in, but who know too much about the company—particularly about its technology and the products that are still in the oven—whom Atari doesn't want to leave, so they're given a million dollars to play around with and instructions not to call too often.)

Apparently, one of Atari's managers whom Atari trained to program and was known around the company as the 90-Day Wonder, went to Ray and told him all his programmers in one of the divisions were useless, and if he was in charge he'd straighten them out. Ray bought it and made him a director of one of Atari's major engineering departments. Three or four months later the programmers approached Ray directly and asked him to get this guy off their backs. Half the programmers had already quit. As group leader he told them not to wear blue jeans or smoke dope. He tried to make them fill out work schedules and do a lot of disciplines a programmer is not accustomed to. The programmers basically told him to take a flying leap Ray. Alan transferred him to R&D.

HARRY JENKINS: I definitely think some people are exiled. I've always been in R&D. A lot of people in R&D come from other places in the company. A lot of our competition, particularly in software, came from Atari. You have a lot of people who are not happy. Many times it's not the fault of upper management but middle management. You get a lousy middle manager who manages people wrong. I've seen a lot of lateral movement into R&D, and I really don't know if it's to get them off what they're doing or because they really want to work in R&D.

ROGER HECTOR: R&D was fun while I was there, no question about it, but I could see the fruitlessness of it all. It is a truly helpless situation—at least it was at the time I was there. We were playing a sort of game of being busy, doing what we "wanted," but the cold reality of it was very little promise, if any, that anything we did would go anywhere. It bothered me, but it probably doesn't bother others. It's like being an author who never gets anything published. Say somebody paid you a lot of money to write and sent you on trips all over the world to do research. You'd travel first class, stay in the best hotels, eat in the best restaurants, dance in the fanciest nightclubs, and there'd be a limousine to make sure you got safely home; and you could just sit there and pour your heart out all over the page, but it would never get published. You can knock any big organization. Atari has skeletons in their closet just like Exxon or Disney. I don't see so much evil, just a lot of incompetence.

12

Rᴀʏ KASSAR'S office is a long rectangle occupying a corner of the top floor of a two-story building at 1265 Bur-regas in Sunnyvale. It is slightly larger than other executive offices at Atari; otherwise nothing distinguishes it as the office of the chairman. There is no art on the walls, no photos, citations or posters—just bare cream-color walls with two windows overlooking the parking lot. The office is spartan, with no distractions. There is a TV, VTR, and some video games, but they are almost always turned off. There's a conference table visible upon entering, and in the corner of the long rectangle, behind his desk, is Ray. He is dressed in an impeccably tailored summer suit. His desk is solid and uncluttered. The issue of *Scientific American* with the chip on the cover is in one of the drawers. On the top of the desk is a jar of Jelly Bellies. Two billion dollars in busi-ness crossed this desk.

The Rise and Fall of Atari

Sitting on the other side of the desk from Ray is a highly respected stock analyst from one of the larger Wall Street brokerages. The firm manages, on commission, their clients' stock market investments. The more money invested and the more productive the stock, the more the firm makes. The main concern is that the stock goes up. The brokerage makes money as its clients made money and as its clients invest more. The analyst's job is to dig up information on companies and pass it along to his investors.

Because of the volatility of the high-technology market, there are certain details the analyst wants to take into consideration before buying stock. Will the market for the company's products increase or decrease? Will the company continue to grow at its current rate? Are the profit margins of its products expanding or shrinking? How much is the company committed to R&D, and what new products are in the works? Will the market be saturated with competitors? Are the managers qualified to run a high-tech company?

Warner made the analyst's job easier by freely supplying him with financial information other companies as successful as Warner don't give out. Analysts attended meetings with Warner/Atari officials, and the really influential analysts attended one-on-ones with Kassar, Warner's co-chief operating officer Manny Gerard, or, if they're really influential, the chairman of the board, Steve Ross. They'd schmooze it up in an office or over breakfast, lunch, or drinks but never over video games.

Some analysts are interested in becoming connected to glamour companies early so it seems that they're experts.

ZAP!

It's easier to become an expert about a glamour company like Atari with a hot product; all the analyst has to do is make up a reason why the company is going to do well. Because the company will do well, no matter what, it seems that the analyst's reason for buying the stock was right, even if it was wrong. A few analysts consistently make a lot of money because they know what they're talking about. In certain cases they know as much about the company as the man running it. As with anything else, when a heads-up analyst with a big brokerage says to buy a stock, other brokers repeat it, until the lowliest broker in a small town, someone who never schmoozed it up with Ray Kassar or Manny Gerard or Steve Ross, is pushing Warner.

Unlike most of his colleagues who had been following Warner since the early seventies, at the height of the pop music explosion, this analyst started following Warner when it bought Atari. In those six years Warner stock rose 3,000 percent.

Ray does not meet with somebody from Wall Street unless someone from Warner, usually Geoff Holmes, the analyst contact at Warner, attends. It took the analyst four months of fits and starts to get this meeting with Ray. He flies out to San Francisco once every three or four months and spends several days meeting with Activision, Imagic, Apple, and a supermarket chain. Both Ray and the analyst are extremely busy, the only time they can meet is on Thursday at 10 A.M.

The analyst establishes the tone of the conversation. Holmes chimes in occasionally, but his is not the dominant voice. Ray is pretty softspoken for a man who is riled most of the time, and his calmness surprises the analyst. The analyst is trying to understand, in the broad sense, where the company is going; whether it's interested in an upper-end game machine; and what research Atari has done to suggest the VCS can get a 50 percent penetration. Ray and Geoff provide figures for current and projected sales, and based on these figures, the analyst predicts a sweet fourth quarter for Warner with earnings up 50 percent.

At the time of the meeting, in the summer of 1982, Atari was a hit factory. There was a video game in 17 percent of American households—up 8 percent from the previous year, and growing. Over the past couple of years Atari has been able to sell as many video games and game players as it produce. The consumer electronics division has turned out a number of best-selling game cartridges, notably Space Invaders, Asteroids, and Pac-Man, which Atari alone sold over two million units. Had Pac-Man been a record, it would have gone platinum.

Pac-Man was adapted from an arcade game developed by Namco. Space Invaders was adapted from an arcade game developed by Taito. Of these three bestsellers, only Asteroids was adapted from an Atari arcade game. Atari doesn't have that many original home video games, which is why many creative engineers left. At the time it didn't seem crucial, because Warner/Atari was a rich company and could continue to license popular arcade games for home video and almost be guaranteed success. Atari's only problem was that it was not producing the volume it could have been selling. Atari wanted to know how many games to produce, so it went to its distributors in October 1981 and asked them to commit to ordering for all of 1982. The distributors, not wanting to be caught short as they had in the past, ordered big.

Based on these orders, Atari geared up for what it was sure would be its greatest hits: E.T. and Raiders of the Lost Ark. The movie *E.T.* had just come out and was already an enormous success, and *Raiders* was one of the biggest movie box-office attractions ever. This was the first time video games were based on films. Before, Atari's strategy meetings had been based on the product it developed, which either worked or didn't. Now Atari was not paying attention to what it was developing; it was counting on the people who saw the movie to buy the game. The feeling around Atari was that they could do no wrong—they didn't see the impending doom. It was like the eve of Pearl Harbor. The officers were in their condominiums, smoking cigars, drinking, and having a good time, while a tidal wave, way out at sea, was getting closer and closer.

* * *

A couple of months after his meeting in Sunnyvale with Ray, the analyst arranged to have breakfast with Manny at the Helmsley Palace in New York. The analyst had met one on one with Manny Gerard a dozen times before. Manny Gerard was really big in the Warner hierarchy, very close to the top. Manny was much coarser than Ray. He was very bright and talked a mile a minute. Every third word was a four-letter expletive. Ray was very refined, unlike Manny. Ray was the type who in a restaurant instantly put his napkin on his lap. He wouldn't sit there with cigar ashes falling all over himself. Ray dined in the finest French restaurants. When the wine captain brought Ray the wine to taste, Ray knew what he was tasting. Manny looked like somebody in a Miller Lite beer commercial. He would be more comfortable grabbing a bite at the Stage Deli. In a loud restaurant, Manny was usually the loudest.

The analyst had met Warner boss Steve Ross many times over the years, at meetings, industry shows, and in restaurants, but he had never spoken to him one on one as he had with Ray Kassar and Manny Gerard. Whenever the dashing, six-foot-four, silver-haired chairman of the board walked into a room, he grabbed everyone's attention. Steve Ross had presence. Often he was flanked by Steven Spielberg on one side and the third Mrs. Ross, the young and beautiful Courtney Sale, on the other. Like Ray Kassar, Steve Ross is always impeccably dressed but in a livelier manner. Embroidered on a pillow in his office is the sentiment, "Living Well is the Best Revenge." He has quite a sense of humor, sometimes bordering on the obnoxious, but he is never so obnoxious that people would not do what he asked. He appears to be someone who might push people to do what he wants them to do, but he never yells at them. They may not like a few of the things he does, but they can't hate him. Warner Communications is a three-billion-dollar corporation and Steve Ross is the Boss.

Twenty minutes before the analyst is to have breakfast

113

with Manny, Manny calls to explain that he's running late and asks if they could meet in his office. The analyst agrees if Manny promises to stay off the phone.

Manny's office occupies a nice chunk of the Rockefeller Center building where Warner has its headquarters, as befits an executive in the office of the president. Memorabilia covers the walls. The office is plush, with lots of distractions. There's a TV, VTR, and some video games, often all going at the same time. Manny is the co-chief operating officer of a multi-billion-dollar conglomerate. Part of his job is to oversee Atari. Atari accounts for 70 percent of Warner's operating profit, including all their divisions, which is to Manny's credit. The consumer electronic division, which is Atari, is earning six times more than Warner's entire record and music publishing division, five times more than its films, and fifty times more than what its Academy Award-winning *Chariots of Fire* grosses.

As impressive as Atari's numbers are, they also show how poorly Warner's other divisions are doing. The movie division did well in the thirties and forties, and their record division did well in the early seventies under Steve Ross. At various times in Warner history, one division carried the corporation, although never on the scale of Atari. It is the story of the tail wagging the dog. Manny acquired this fledgling video game company for a measly $28 million, and now it's worth $2 billion. If Atari were an independent company and not a subsidiary wholly owned by Warner, it would have ranked around 300 on the *Fortune* 500.

When Manny and the analyst met, the first thing they

did was compliment each other. Ray and the analyst had complimented each other indirectly; the figures they had thrown around were complimentary. Manny complimented the analyst because he wanted to impress him. The analyst complimented Manny because he wanted inside information.

Manny loves to snow people, but he's also very smart, which makes him very endearing, even if he's a loudmouth. The analyst was predicting that Warner would finish the year at $5^1/_4$, with earnings up 50 percent over the previous year, and Manny was confirming those figures. Over the weeks following the meeting with Manny, the analyst called to verify those figures with his contact at Warner, who confirmed them as late as December 7, 1982. Therefore at 3:04 P.M. Eastern Standard Time, the analyst was shocked and furious when an announcement came across the wire in his office: Warner, citing a slump in Atari sales, expected only a 10 to 15 percent increase in earnings for the fourth quarter.

The following day Warner stock plummeted $16^3/_4$ points, one-third their value, from $51^7/_8$ to $35^1/_8$ and closed the quarter with profits down 56 percent, Warner's first decline in nearly eight years.

*   *   *

It was probably pretty wild around Atari/Warner three or four days before December 8. They didn't suddenly look at something out of the computer and say, "Oh our sales are lower than we thought," and call the press immediately.

There must have been a period of time when they were worrying about what they were going to do.

Steve Ross no doubt thought that Manny Gerard was on top of the situation; Manny thought Ray Kassar was on top of it; Ray thought Perry Odak, president of consumer electronics and the number-four man, was on top of it; and for a time it seemed everybody was on top of it. This was a chain of command where the number-four man, the president of a major division, would be the number-one man in most companies. Ray was probably the first to analyze the situation and realize there was no solution. The others probably would have tried to talk around, gloss over, or deny the problem out of existence.

When Atari told its distributors in October 1981 to order for all of 1982 in one shot, Atari dominated 80 percent of the video game market and assumed it would always be that way. But if Atari had looked more closely at what was going on, it would have had very good reason to believe things would change.

Mattel, which sold 200,000 Intellivisions in 1980, and was a distant second behind Atari, had tripled its output and began marketing Intellivisions aggressively. Then Coleco, which everybody thought had dropped out of the picture in 1979 when it lost fortunes with hand-held electronic games during the video invasion, stunned everyone with ColecoVision, which came out of the box like gangbusters.

Intellivision and ColecoVision were the first of the so-called second generation video game systems. The figures on the screen looked more like shapes than sticks. Baseballs were round, not square, and rolled across the screen. The three-hundred-dollar price tag was worth it. Atari's primitive one-hundred-eighty-dollar VCS hadn't changed since 1976.

While Mattel and Coleco challenged Atari's hardware, small, hungry, highly innovative upstarts, led by Activision and Imagic, attacked Atari's software with second-generation video games like Pit Fall and Freeway. Suddenly the market was filled with games, and Atari's monopoly disappeared. Everybody in the industry was forced to cut prices. Not only was Atari selling less, but it was also making less on what it sold.

In October 1982 Atari had three of the five top-selling games on *Billboard*'s video game chart. In December they had only one, Berserk, and if it hadn't been so heavily advertised—it was one of those ads in which the graphics in the commercial were more exciting than the graphics of the actual game—it may not even have made fourth place. E.T. and Raiders of the Lost Ark didn't come close to making the list.

In addition to ColecoVision, Coleco made the wise decision to license Donkey Kong, which was almost as big a hit in the arcades as Pac-Man. If Coleco hadn't licensed Donkey Kong, Atari would have, and Coleco might not have done so well. Licensing a popular arcade game is a trick Coleco picked up from Atari but Mattel didn't.

Coleco succeeded in picking the right arcade game for the time. It could have been off by two weeks and never have made a dime. It also licensed Frogger and Mousetrap, which are not talked about as much as Donkey Kong but are really good games. Mattel can talk about how advanced its system is and how realistic its sporting games are in general, but it never had a specific hit game, like Pac-Man or Donkey Kong, to identify it.

Like Activision and Imagic, Coleco made its software compatible with the VCS and Intellivision. It even added a wrinkle. It developed a new piece of technology called a module, which when plugged into ColecoVision could play Atari's, Activision's and Imagic's best games. It probably wasn't developed so much to be sold as to be talked about. What Coleco and everybody else wants is for somebody to go out and buy its product. Somebody might buy ColecoVision thinking they could buy an adapter and play whatever game was hot. The majority of people who went out and bought ColecoVision with the idea they would buy the adapter later will probably never buy it, which is to Coleco's advantage if they bought software from Coleco. In any event, people stopped buying Atari.

The reason one game cartridge doesn't fit all game players and computers—and why there's a need for the module—is because the mechanism that the cartridge slips into varies from machine to machine. When the record industry began, the first record players on the market played at different speeds. People had to buy records at the speed their record player revolved at. Records were made to be played at either 16 rpm's, 33$\frac{1}{3}$ rpm's, 45 rpm's, or 78 rpm's. Often the same companies made both records and record players. After a decade or so Columbia, the biggest record manufacturer, and who also made record players, got together with Victrola, the biggest record player manufacturer who also made records, and the two agreed to split up the market. Victrola would produce the hardware and Columbia the software. $33^1/_3$ was the standard speed. The other companies followed. It is still too early in the video game industry for companies battling it out like Atari, Coleco and Intellivision to standardize. They probably never will because the video game industry won't be as enduring as the record industry.

In late 1982 Atari finally came out with its second-generation 5200, which was actually the Atari 400 home computer repackaged. The significant difference between the 5200 and the VCS is the 5200's greater amount of memory, which means better graphics, more action, and more sophisticated games. The new joystick moved 360 degrees, making it easier to maneuver.

But all the advantages gave way to the fact that when it came out the 5200 was incompatible with Atari's most profitable VCS game cartridges. The VCS's success had little to do with the VCS itself. People bought the console so they could play Atari games. When Coleco and Mattel added modules, making their consoles compatible with Atari cartridges, there was no binding reason to buy the 5200 rather than ColecoVision or Intellivision.

That summer, while the analyst was meeting with Ray Kassar in Sunnyvale, the first cancellations came trickling in. By the time the analyst met with Manny Gerard in New York two months later, the number of cancellations had become significant. The analyst believed the Warner spokesman when he said Warner did not know its own figures. Had somebody at Warner sat down and taken a hard look at those cancellations around November 1, they would have come out with a number well below the $5\frac{1}{4}$ they were projecting.

It's possible that in obtaining inside information, the analyst, Ray, and Manny became too chummy and lost their objectivity. Warner was feeding the analyst projections based partly on the assumption that Atari would sell all the products its distributors had ordered back in October, as they had in the past, and partly on what Wall Street and the media were saying. At the time, analysts, especially those who chased glamour stocks, were hyping Atari to Atari. They were saying, "Gee, we figure you're going to do $5\frac{1}{4}$ a share." What was Warner going to say? It was probably news to them.

"We were dumb," Manny admitted to the analyst. "We never had to face cancellations or such competition before." He swore he didn't know about the cancellations until the announcement.

Obviously, someone at Atari knew sales were in trouble before it was announced. Somebody in sales must have been receiving those cancellations. Someone in manufacturing must have seen E.T., Raiders of the Lost Ark, and their other products come off the assembly line and pile up in bins in big numbers, where they remained after the orders were canceled. There must have been some information that could have been passed up the chain of command; but, instead, it was closely guarded.

Maybe someone saw it coming all along, but it was so awful he couldn't tell anyone. A fairly responsible person in the company who didn't know what was happening may have stumbled on to the problem and told a fairly important but not responsible person who, because it would be his neck on the line, sat on it. Maybe he figured, with E.T. about to come out, Atari would recover at a higher level and pull it out.

But Atari didn't pull it out. Eventually, whoever that person at Atari was, was eliminated. That's why it looks like it was Perry Odak. Was it a coincidence that Warner announced Odak was being removed from his position as president of consumer electronics, the biggest of Atari's three divisions, later the same day Warner announced earnings would be a lot less than they had been confirming? If Odak had been a great asset to the company, Warner would not have announced his removal the same day. They would have waited a month. Giving the president of a major division the ax is not something a company does to get favorable publicity. They must have done it because they really wanted to get rid of him. Or they wanted to make him the scapegoat so it looked like they had found the reason for their trouble and had gotten rid of it.

The analyst had attended formal meetings with Perry Odak back in the summer, and had thought him "the biggest clown he'd ever met." Odak, who came from Jovan, the perfume company, was raving about Atari's great software strategy and how unique it was, while Geoff Holmes, the analyst contact, was sitting right next to him and most of the analysts at the meeting had already seen these products and weren't impressed.

Now take a look at the original Atari chain of command. Nolan Bushnell was on top, followed by Joe Keenan, Al Alcorn, Steve Bristow, and Gene Lipkin. Most had beards and looked like Smith Brothers. Joe Keenan was the only straight-looking one and the only one who looked like he would fit in with the Ross-Gerard-Kassar crowd. Maybe that's why Nolan hired him. He could have been the corporate image Nolan needed. The others—Ross, Gerard, Kassar— had corporate image but not the foggiest notion of how to make a video game or of the technology Atari was founded on, so they better have been good at something.

What was it they *were* good at? Everyone thought it was marketing. It wasn't marketing, because if it were, E.T. and Raiders wouldn't have bombed. Atari became as successful as a company could get, but it happened very fast, right after Nolan and the others left. For the Warner regime to use their marketing expertise, they needed a product and a strategy, and one suspects they had neither.

13

WARNER eventually closed the quarter reporting only 3.96, yet it was endorsing 5.25 a week before the announcement. But about three weeks before the shocker there were enough inuendos bothering the analyst that his estimates started going south. Instead of predicting $5^1/_4$, he came down to 5. No one on Wall Street had any idea Warner was going to report a buck less than they had been confirming.

THE ANALYST: One thing that bothered me concerned Knickerbocker, a toy company Warner bought several years ago. Over the years I became good friends with the president of Hasbro, and Hasbro was essentially taking Knickerbocker off Warner's hands. The president was suggesting how mismanaged Knickerbocker was. They set up a large staff in the Orient—about five times as large as they needed—and overpaid middle management people. The company was generally in a state of disarray. If this in fact was going on at Knickerbocker, I wondered what was going on at Atari. It didn't occur to me then that what was going on at Atari was worse than what was going on at Knickerbocker.

As Atari became more of a marketing and manufacturing company, Kassar forced out many of the creative, free-wheeling, and loosely organized engineers and replaced them with veteran sales and marketing execs from big corporations like Jovan, Kodak, and American Can, who, like himself, didn't know the video game business. The problem was that they were leaving faster than the engineers.

Two weeks prior to Perry Odak's dismissal, a senior VP of sales and marketing in the same department was discharged after eight months on the job, and a VP of field sales for that division, the man probably in the best position in the world to know just how well sales were going, was canned after two months. The presidents of Atari's two other divisions—coin-op and home computer—quit during the summer. Manny Gerard said Warner accepted the huge turnover as a consequence of what happened when Atari grew tenfold in the four years since Ray Kassar had taken charge.

Many of those leaving Atari attributed the high turnover directly to Kassar's autocratic managing style. One former VP of marketing complained that Kassar placed strong-minded professionals in decision-making positions but never let them make decisions. That many people can't make decisions all the time, particularly if they are top bananas in their field. Take twenty of the best people in any field, put them together in the same office, and they won't be able to do anything, especially if part of their expertise is calling the shots. Unless, by some miracle, they all agree on the same shot, eventually only one of them is going to have the power and nineteen are going to be irate. Although Atari's executives knew how to call shots, they knew nothing about computers. They had no idea what could be done with them. They called their shots based on things their engineers told them, which they might not really have understood. One president, of an electronics division, might have known what he was doing, but he may have had to get approval first from other executives who didn't, so they sent him from one to the other until the last one told him not to do anything for awhile.

It might not have happened that neatly. Somebody might have obtained approval for an idea and everybody working on the project got excited, until somebody from the highest echelon came down and told them to forget it. Sometimes one executive is capable of wiping out the efforts of an entire engineering department single-handedly, and at Atari Ray Kassar certainly had that power.

A week after Warner stock plummeted, Wall Street was rocked by the insider trading scandal involving Ray Kassar and another Atari associate, and the analyst just threw up his arms in disgust.

Ray Kassar sold 5,000 Warner shares at about 11:41 A.M., Pacific Standard Time, 23 minutes before the announcement. After conducting a nine-month investigation, the Securities and Exchange Commission alleged that Kassar had based his action on illegal insider information not known to the public. Did Kassar assure those high figures so the worth of his stock would go up when he sold it? Was Kassar, who was earning more than a million dollars a year, that stupid? Was it year-end tax planning, and had he told his broker a couple of weeks prior to the announcement that if the broker had a certain target price, he was to sell?

Ray may not have been manipulating the stock, although he may have known what was going to happen three days sooner than anybody else. Obviously he knew a little sooner. The announcement didn't come over the wire in his office, as it did in the offices of the stockbrokers.

Neither admitting nor denying the charges, Kassar agreed to turn over $81,875, representing the profit he made by selling when he did, rather than being inconvenienced and embarrassed by going to court. Dennis Groth, a senior vice president at Atari, also accused of inside trading, vowed to vigorously defend against the charges.

Several weeks before the sale, Kassar had issued to the organization a book with his picture on the cover, describing certain rules of ethical conduct, one concerned with insider sales. Warner's position was that while an SEC investigation was going on, they would have agreed to anything the SEC said. The analyst would have liked it if Manny Gerard or Steve Ross had sat down with Ray, to find out what the hell had happened and judge him. In the meantime Ray was not suspended, pending SEC findings. He just couldn't talk to anyone. He had lawyers buttoning him up.

Ray was being paid a lot of money. He still had a lot of power. He was running a company where they could hire the best. Warner certainly had the capital and the glamour to attract the best. While running the company, Kassar sold a lot of VCS's and a number of hit games, but it isn't clear whether the VCS sold because of Kassar or due to the incredible success of Space Invaders. Maybe anyone could have walked in there and accomplished as much as Ray Kassar did. Ray could have tripped on his way to work the first day, and by the time he was out of the hospital, all the sales could already have been happening. If the world had stopped in mid-1982, Ray Kassar would have gone down in history as a genius, one of the shrewdest businessmen to come down the pike.

Whether Ray deserves credit for the VCS or not, he was hired to run the company. Atari wanted to be around more than a year and a half. Ray was in the position to assure that. Although Atari's rise was very steep, it had a relatively low vantage point. It was like being at the North Pole: You are at the top of the world, but when you look out at the vast emptiness surrounding you, you feel as if you are a speck on an infinite plane. Ray Kassar was like a man on a really big roller coaster, where it takes a long time to get from the point where the roller coaster comes to a stop to the point where it starts going down.

If Ray had really been on the ball, Atari wouldn't have been in the trouble it was in. Ray might have been very good at selling products, but he wasn't good at developing

ZAP!

them. Maybe somebody else should have been the top man, and then when Atari came up with something interesting he could have said, "Here Ray, go out and sell it."

* * *

Warner had made a tremendous effort to take credit for Atari's phenomenal success and to discredit Nolan. Now there was nothing for Warner to take credit for. Warner stock prices hadn't risen much since plunging 40 percent on December 9. A year earlier, at an extravagant reception in Las Vegas, Steve Ross and his buddy Frank Sinatra mingled among the throng of euphoric Atari dealers. Atari controlled 75% of the home video game market, accounted for half of Warner's $4 billion in revenues and more than 60% of its operating net. Atari had shipped $98 million worth of game cartridges in the week before Thanksgiving (1982). A week-and-a-half later, they didn't ship any. Many of those jovial dealers were cancelling. At the 1983 annual stockholders' meeting, Ross announced that, because of the Atari problem, he expected Warner to report second-quarter losses to be worse than the $18.9 million first-quarter deficit. Warner closed the 1983 second-quarter losing $283.4 million, which was three times worse than what the analyst was predicting. It was, in fact, the worse quarter in Warner history. Ross assured the stockholders that the company was thoroughly investigating what really had happened at Atari; it would have been more reassuring had Warner already investigated the problem and come up with the solution.

In light of the eighteen class-action suits filed by stockholders charging Warner with failure to announce Atari's problems sooner than it did, Ross insisted he had disclosed them the moment he had heard about them. He said the cancellations were "the most amazing thing" he had ever heard.

Unfortunately, Atari was not his only problem. Warner's troubles began around Thanksgiving 1982 and got worse as the year went by. On November 23, Gustave Hauer had resigned as chairman of Warner-Amex Cable Communications, the cable TV company Warner owns jointly with American Express, which it was estimated would lose between thirty and forty million dollars in 1982. Hauer's post was taken over by former Transportation Secretary Drew Lewis, and Gerard, in an attempt to pacify impatient stockholders, promised that Warner-Amex would pay off in spades by 1985.

On November 24 Warner agreed in principle to sell certain assets of its Knickerbocker Toy division to Hasbro Industries. Knickerbocker was expected to fall short by twenty or thirty million dollars on Warner's *Dukes of Hazzard* toy products when, as Gerard put it, "One morning in August *Dukes of Hazzard* went off the cliff."

On November 27 Solomon Weiss, former assistant treasurer at Warner, was convicted of fraud, racketeering, and perjury. He was found guilty of buying stock in the Westchester Premier Theatre in Tarrytown in exchange for a $170,000 bribe, which was stashed away in a secret slush fund. Jay Emmett, a former member of the office of the president, and Leonard Horwitz, a former sixty-thousand-dollar-a-year consultant, received suspended sentences in exchange for their crucial cooperation in nailing Weiss. A number of mobsters had been convicted earlier in a related case, and the theater went bankrupt. Nick Akerman, the federal prosecutor, stunned the packed courtroom at the sentencing of the two when he asserted "that the real culprit" was the chairman of the board of Warner, Steve Ross.

Although this series of events was clearly Warner's headache and had nothing to do with Atari, it would have been hard to separate the two in the minds of stockholders.

The role of Steve Ross in the Atari problem was hard to figure. Many analysts and stockholders blamed the mess at Warner in general on Steve Ross and his decentralized policies and laissez-faire approach. It was the same thing Warner had criticized Nolan for. Nolan thought Warner's problem was too much control, not too little. "Steve Ross's theories," said Nolan, "didn't permeate down to the intermediate levels. The same things that caused Warner to flourish caused Atari to perish."

Steve Ross was on the analyst's black list. He'd been trying for nine months to arrange a meeting with Ross, and he was incensed that he couldn't get to see him. Most people in business seemed to think the analyst knew what he was doing and returned his calls within an hour. It usually took Ray a week to return his calls and Manny ten days; his calls to Ross went unreturned.

THE ANALYST: There's a relatively formal system that's been established in the U.S. equity market, where the analyst has a job to do that calls for him to do a fair amount of communication with top executives. Companies have to communicate with their shareholders, and the best way is through their annual report, quarterly statements, and meetings with analysts. Ross in this respect is more arrogant than Kassar, which is unusual if not uncommon for a company that views itself as a public company through and through. I know the layers and layers of secretaries you have to go through to get to Ross. The irony is the second word of this corporation's name. They communicate as poorly as any company I have ever known.

Atari was a phenomenon of real success for about a year and a half. The marketing was blossoming, but the analyst had a lot of questions about the last year of that year and a half. If he could have sat down with Steve Ross, the last thing he would have done was waste his time with compliments. He would have asked how Ross could have had a division that contributed 70 percent of Warner's earnings and overbuilt inventory by twenty million units and not have any knowledge of it.

According to the analyst, the company was in a very severe inventory bind. They had about ten million dollars' worth of finished goods in Taiwan for which there were no customers, and they had five million pieces and parts for the E.T. game, which wasn't moving either. They had sold a million units and had five million more they had expected to sell unassembled on the shelves, and there was a big logjam in the supply pipeline of games.

ZAP!

Atari is a classic example of a company where nobody seemed to know what they were doing; certainly not the people in control. They were blinded by their own success. They *thought* they were in control. The designers of many of Atari's best products left. Either these designers, or Kassar, had made Atari, not the legions Kassar brought in.

Atari didn't know what it was doing in October 1981 when all their distributors were told to order for all of 1982. The people in control didn't know what they were doing when they produced so many E.T. games. They didn't know what they were doing when they lost market share. If they had known, those top executives wouldn't have quit or been fired soon after they arrived. More top engineers would have stuck around. They would have been able to come up with more successful products.

Part of Atari's downfall was that there was no product. That's why they lost share. It wasn't because of competition. If that had been the case, they should have been developing something else. Maybe they are now; but maybe it's too late. There should have been continuity. Atari could bring out a new game or game player or a nonvideo game product that will put Atari back on top, but right now they're not necessarily in a good position to do that, at least they are not in a better position than anyone else to do that.

14

WHEN Warner announced that its profits would be off, it wasn't only Warner stock that took a beating. The whole industry was affected, although not to the same degree; but then they weren't all market share leaders. Atari was.

Mattel had a better year in 1982 than in 1981. It suffered a loss in that fourth quarter but not due, as Atari claimed, to any slump in sales that was industrywide. Intellivision's sales were up. Their loss could be attributed to the high cost of their George Plimpton television commercials. Coleco reported ColecoVision sales had increased sixfold, from $34.9 million to $203.3 million, and their fourth-quarter earnings were $15.3 million. A year before they had shown a $661,000 loss. Coleco's gain in market share, which would stabilize at 15 percent, meant a loss for the other companies. Companies' ultimate market shares and how they get there—whether they're growing or declining—indicate who will realize earning growth and who won't.

ZAP!

THE ANALYST: When Warner stock broke at 31, there was no reason, from a trading point of view, to buy Warner; but, as I told my clients, if you close your eyes and open them a year later, Atari could turn it around. Atari has a game development project with LucasFilm, where Atari manufactures games designed by the director of Star Wars. That could turn out to be quite interesting. The deal with MCA, giving Atari the right to develop any of MCA's upcoming movies into games, could pan out. But what impresses me most is that Kassar brought in talent like Alan Kay and Ted Hoff. They're the best salesmen at Warner Communications.

Ray Kassar snatched Kay from Xerox, where he headed the learning research group. One project at Xerox had kids animating Saturday morning cartoons with electronic paint brushes instead of just passively watching them. Kassar made Kay chief scientist, and he now heads an R&D program at Atari that runs up a hundred-million-dollar tab every year. Kay said that when he took the job he received two directives: Gerard told him to take risks; Kassar told him to dream.

THE ANALYST: I met Alan Kay twice. I'm not sure if Kay has the world's best track record for new products; he's probably one of fifty or a hundred around the country who has such qualifications. Beyond him, I'm amazed by Atari's inability to do much product development stuff. When I look around the industry I see Coleco with a better video game

*system and shipping more than Atari is. And Commodore,
who doesn't have much R&D other than their own chip
company, is coming out consistently with better products
and a better price value than Atari. The fact that none of
the Atari or Warner brass has any electronics background
is no excuse, because Coleco management doesn't have
any either, but somehow they've designed the right product
for the market.*

The analyst had not met Ted Hoff yet. Ray may have hired
Hoff, who invented the microprocessor while at Intel, because he had Intel written across his forehead. Intel is a very
big, comparatively well-run company with a lot of prestige.
If it wasn't, IBM, which is the most prestigious and best-run
company, wouldn't have bought into it.

IBM announced they were buying into Intel to protect
the American electronics market from the Japanese. They
could have put their money into Texas Instruments or Atari.
Obviously, Intel manufactures the chips IBM uses, but that's
not all Intel does. There are a lot of electronics companies.
IBM could have put their money into National Semiconductor, but they bought into Intel.

IBM's reason, which most people believe, is that they
were protecting their source of supply and technology; but
as important as IBM is, Intel is the trendsetter. If something
should happen to Intel, if they were bought by a Japanese
company, for instance, that would be the end of the American semiconductor development. If Japan had the edge in
semiconductor technology, Japanese computer companies

would have a distinct advantage over IBM. That's certainly one reason why IBM bought Intel. IBM doesn't have a history of taking over competing companies. They'd rather wipe them out completely.

*   *   *

IBM is a company that hit the top and stayed there. IBM has never fallen. It's had times when it hasn't been as strong as at other times, but it has never been in trouble.

IBM did not have the growth rate of Atari. Although IBM is worth quite a bit more than Atari, it's not how much it's worth but for how long it's been worth what it's worth. IBM is a blue-chip stock. People put their money into IBM because the chances of losing their money are very slim. On the other hand, the chances of making a windfall are just as slim. IBM stock is not going to go up 3,000 percent like Warner. But Warner, even with Atari, is not a blue-chip stock. It's a glamour stock. Or it was. It might have been— and still might become—a blue chip, but so far it hasn't.

The atmosphere at IBM is what is to be expected from a respectable, New England, blue-chip company. The atmosphere at IBM has never been as good as the atmosphere once was at Atari, and it has never been as bad as the atmosphere at Atari is now. IBM is run in a controlled, studious way. The man driving that thing is named John Opel. There's no one from another company looking over his shoulder. There's no Gerard or Warner. IBM owns IBM. There's no big turnover. It puts a lot of money into research and doesn't do anything suddenly. No matter what.

The Rise and Fall of Atari

IBM also tends to design things so that it has the consumer trapped in IBM. Atari does that, too, but not so successfully. IBM is very good at it, but it's easier at the high end of the market, where cost is not quite so important as it is lower down.

IBM has an extraordinary reputation, but what's most impressive about it is that it went into personal computers very late—almost the last company in—and in a year it had the majority share of the market. And they're not even competing on the low end of the market. They designed a product that wasn't bad. It wasn't a breakthrough, but it was good; there was really nothing wrong with it. Also, it had "IBM" on it. That helped a lot. If either one of those two factors were not true, IBM might not have captured a majority share, but since they both were true, it did, which is very different from Atari. Atari felt it could do anything it wanted to, just because it was Atari.

IBM is fairly ruthless. If they feel someone's gaining on them, they step on them, and much more effectively than Atari. When IBM steps on someone, they get squashed.

*　　*　　*

1983 could be the last big year of growth in the industry. It's going to be a flat industry, predicts the analyst. Some analysts think 30 percent of American homes will have some kind of video game by 1984, which is up from 17 percent in 1982. But then profits will fall off sharply in 1984 as revenue growth fades and margin pressures intensify. By 1986 everyone who can afford and wants a video game will have one, and manufacturers will have to drop their prices further. Heavy competition will drive marketing and promotional expenses up. And the quality will suffer; the systems will probably be so crummy that nobody will want a video game anymore.

Any further growth at Atari and in the video game industry generally, in terms of selling units and bringing in earnings, is going to come from overseas. Mabye 40 or 45 percent of revenues will come from an overseas market. There are still a lot of households in Africa, Asia, Europe, and South America without a home video game system. Maybe Atari will do well overseas. Jerry Lewis movies do very well overseas. Charles Bronson is a monster abroad. Maybe Atari will do well overseas and lousy here. What they could do is dump the stuff there they can't sell here, which would postpone the inevitable. But that's no way to build a company. If Atari continued to do well here and then did well over there, that would be very good.

How well anyone's home video system does will depend on how quickly personal computers take over the video game market and in what numbers. Everyone knows personal computers will ultimately be a larger market than video games. People are already calling the personal computer "P.C.," as if it were a TV.

There were one- to one-and-a-half million households with personal computers in 1982, and that number is expected to reach ten million by 1986. Of those million to a-million-and-a-half computers, three quarters were low-end. That included Atari's 400, Texas Instruments' 99/4A, Commodore's VIC-20, and the Tandy TRS-80, which were predominantly used to play video games. Even among high-end Apple II owners, over 60 percent of the software bought were games.

Low-end video game players, like the VCS, probably won't be threatened by the P.C. until 1985. It's the high-end and trade-up segment of the market—Intellivision, ColecoVision, and Atari 5200—that's worried, since the upper income, educated household is also the target for the personal computer. That target should get bigger as the discounting on personal computers increases. In mid-1983 a P.C. cost as little as the VCS. The VCS, once basically the *only* game player, started out at $150 above average.

There's no way a video game company like Atari can compete with the personal computer. No technological improvements can be made on the game console that can't be duplicated by computers, because the game *is* a computer. The graphics on a computer are better, and there's no reason why the graphics on the home computer will ever be better than the home computer. It goes without saying that the home video game can't be made more like a computer than a computer.

Since video game companies can't compete with the P.C.'s hardware, the only way companies like Atari, Mattel, and Coleco can succeed is through software. The question is, which one of the current game companies will be first to sink its hooks into the new burgeoning market. Atari has established product strength, software support, and distribution over the other video game companies. In a very narrow sense, Atari may seem to be the video game company that is going to do best in the personal computer market; but if you look to see which video game company is going to do well in the personal computer market, the answer is none of them. No video game company is going to do as well as IBM, Apple, Commodore, or Radio Shack.

* * *

Software-only companies like Activision and Imagic will probably benefit from the emerging computer software market, but not at the margin they've been enjoying. In 1982 software out-revenued hardware for the first time, making it the most competitive market in the industry. It takes almost no overhead to produce software. All it requires are an idea for a game and a program. A big company's only advantage is in distribution and advertising, not the game itself. There are a lot of people who can program, and the best programmers aren't necessarily at the biggest companies. Judging by relative sales, these programmers aren't at Atari.

A lot of programmers are fairly young and haven't entered the job market yet. Atari can't go out and hire up everybody. Quite frequently somebody's going to come up with something in his garage and sell it to whoever makes him the best offer. Having a big office at Atari or Activision and a large R&D budget is absolutely no advantage in being able to produce the best software. All anyone has to do is go out and buy an Atari 800 computer, and they can write programs for an Atari video game. For a thousand dollars someone can set himself up to write programs, and if he or she is going to school, even elementary school, the skills can be developed for free. If a company were consistently turning out good software, the fact that they had momentum and marketing facilities would give them an advantage, but Atari doesn't turn out consistently good software. If Atari were the only people making software, then they would have it sewn up. But they aren't. Somebody goes out, buys a VIC-20 or Atari 800, and then goes down to the local computer store. For twenty dollars he can buy a disc that has a game on it that is three times as exciting as Atari's most exciting cartridge. Not only that, he'll be able to make a copy of that game and give it to his friends, and the only company that will benefit is the one that makes blank video cartridges.

*   *   *

Atari started out as a coin-op company, and to a certain extent coin-op is still an important operation to Atari. The people who have been around Atari the longest are all coin-op people. Coin-op is a very significant accent on the entire company, but people often overlook it. They think the coin-op business is saturated, that it's going into the tank, and Atari's probably going to shuck it off.

In early 1983 Atari laid off 1,700 workers and moved manufacturing of home computers and home video games from Sunnyvale and San Jose to Hong Kong and Taiwan. The joke is that Atari moved to a plant offshore where they could hide all this stuff they didn't sell. They didn't move production of coin-op. The reason is that they looked on this division as part of their creative R&D effort. The reason Atari gave for moving their other manufacturing offshore was to cut overhead.

Bally's Midway is expected to be the leader in coin-op games, but their earnings, which in 1982 accounted for 85 percent of Bally's total profits, are shrinking along with the arcade market. The analyst expects the coin-operated market, which doubled in growth rate in 1980 and 1981 but was down in 1982 and 1983, to improve as new game technology is developed. Major research is now going on in enhanced graphic resolution, reaching almost photo-realism, and 3-D and holographic images. The technology for these games is already there; the price isn't.

There's already a graphics technology that can't be beat, called video discs. There are already video disc coin-op games available that don't *approach* photo-realism; they *are* photo-realism. There are games in development that are animated cartoons, and there are games that run like a motion picture: what happens to the characters depends on the player. These games are cost-effective; they don't run into the expense of producing a high-resolution, *computer-generated* image. The computer doesn't even generate the image, so a high-speed computer, which is extremely expensive, isn't needed. An enormous amount of memory isn't required to hold the image because it's on the video disc. No doubt, video games that aren't on video discs will come along that will knock everybody over. They will stir a new interest in specific video games. There will be little peaks, but if you draw a straight line through the center of the peaks, you'll see that it's going downhill.

The Rise and Fall of Atari

*   *   *

In the end, the video game may be just another Hula Hoop, although the sheer number of video games would argue against it. The twenty-or-so-million video games in people's homes and the billions of quarters spent in arcades do say something about the innate attraction of this form of entertainment. Video game makers such as Atari would never get this kind of penetration if they were fly-by-night operations.

People still have Hula Hoops—although maybe not as many as once did—and there are people who will hold on to their video games. Fads come and go, and it's this coming and going that keeps industries going. First the miniskirt, then the maxi. Some fads peak at such heights that it becomes impossible to predict when the bottom will fall out. That's what happened to the CB radio. It became so popular, so fast, that by the time most companies jumped in, it was too late. The opposite happened to Atari. At first, others thought it would be another CB, and for ten years Atari had the market practically to itself before everybody else caught on. Video games are as significant as TV, and Atari put the TV viewer in the driver's seat. That in itself is significant. The viewer is no longer the passenger, watching the scenery roll by. Now the TV screen is passive and the viewer active. The viewer takes the wheel, gives it gas, breaks, steals second base, falls into a pit, catches the baby falling out of the burning building, patrols the planet, heads off alien invaders, removes the malignant tumor.

Perhaps Atari's most significant contribution is that it

paved the way for the personal computer, which is not a fad. If nothing else, video games have prepared the world for the computer age. A computer is, after all, a video game, except it's smarter. It has more memory, works faster, draws better graphics, and does things besides play games. That's a lot more than you can say about a Hula Hoop. Had Wham-O had Hula Hoops and nothing else, that would have been it for them. But Wham-O followed with Frisbee, whereas Atari's video games led to somebody else's computer, not necessarily Atari's. In that sense, Wham-O did better than Atari.

Atari could still possibly pull out of the hole. The deal with LucasFilms, where Geroge "Star Wars" Lucas creates a video game that Atari licenses, could work out. Something could become of all the R&D money Atari has tied up with Evans and Southerland, a company known for the high-quality computer graphics it designs for flight simulators. Maybe Hoff and Kay will make profitable innovations. Atari could come up with a game that utilizes holographic and three-dimensional technology, one that allows a player to step inside as one would the cockpit of a jet plane or a rocket ship. There's an instrument panel and lots of buttons and video screens all around you, and when you drop your money into the the coin slot you have the sensation that you're actually flying. Atari could come up with the greatest video game imaginable, and yet a new fad that has nothing to do with Atari or video games could come along, and, zap, no more video games. Or, in another scenario, Atari, unable to make a comeback, could be sold or shut down

The Rise and Fall of Atari

by Warner; or Warner could suffer a hostile takeover—and, zap, no more Atari.

Bell Laboratories might very well do something interesting that will become the next fad. Bell Labs did invent the transistor; and it did all the important laser work; and it does have a big, well-stocked laboratory in New Jersey. It's a leader in its field, which is the electronics industry, period. And it really hasn't been into consumer electronics, except for the telephone, which has remained substantially the same for fifty or sixty years.

But now Bell's into consumer products. Bell doesn't own local telephone companies anymore. It's given that up, which it probably didn't want to do. But it no longer is barred from competing against personal computer or data processing companies. For the right to be the only people who could provide phone service, they had to give up other rights, but they don't have to do that anymore. A.T.&T. is free to enter the video game market. It made a deal with Coleco to develop a system that delivers video games over the telephone wires to subscribers, like video Muzak. Video games will be just one of many lines A.T.&T. expects to get into. They're really quite expert in the field of consumer information. Presumably they have a nice working relationship with the companies they're about to divest: all the local phone companies.

Suppose the next big fad is home information services, through which shopping and making travel reservations can be done at home on a little terminal. Bell is well connected—they're used to running wires into homes, and their wires

145

are designed for transforming information. Also, Bell is very good at retailing to the entire population of the United States. They are the biggest retailer in the country, if not the world. Their talent isn't limited to making communication products, they make the best communication products. They're used to making things in a big way. They make massive quantities of stuff, and their stuff works. They don't make code-breakers, build missiles, or send people to the moon, but they do make things for defense, and they do make things for rocketships.

Although a communications company like Bell is not an entertainment company like Warner, it can leap-frog the entertainment industry. People can be entertained by something outside the entertainment market; it's just a question of how you define entertainment. 1980 through 1982 were the years of the entertainment market as far as video games were concerned, and the video game phase of the entertainment market made a lot of money. Eight years before that the entertainment market made money on records, and in the forties and fifties the entertainment market was making big money in pictures. But in between those boom times the entertainment market wasn't doing that well. Look at what people spend their money on. If there were a neat little terminal and it put people in touch with everything they wanted to be in touch with, people would stop playing video games.

15

TWO WEEKS after leaving Atari, Nolan Bushnell went into the pizza parlor business. Nolan isn't Italian, but he knew the worst part about pizza is waiting twenty minutes with nothing to do while the pizza's in the oven. So he stuck a hundred video games in the next room, and those twenty minutes became intensely profitable. Nolan didn't want to run just any pizza parlor. He'd had visions of showing the world how to run an arcade since his amusement park days. An oversized rat named Chuck E. Cheese, a piano-playing hippopotamus, and the other robots were just a gimmick. To make Pizza Time Theater a family restaurant, Nolan had to balance the video arcade with wholesome entertainment.

While Nolan was sitting in a Pizza and Pipes restaurant in Redwood City, California, in 1973, he realized how well Wurlitzer organ music goes with pizza. Then it struck him that he could provide better entertainment using robots.

ZAP!

Robots are cheaper than live entertainers, so he ordered the engineers at Atari to build and program six Pizza Time Players to perform three-minute skits every eight minutes.

The idea for the animal characters came when he picked up an eight-hundred-dollar costume of what looked like a coyote at an industry show and gave it to his engineers with instructions to make it talk and sing. Nolan was hoping to get back a Mickey Mouse, someone with star qualities kids could easily recognize, and he got back Chuck E. Cheese, Pizza Time's mascot and Nolan's alter ego.

Pizza Time Theater was one of those wacky ideas developed at Grass Valley and not destroyed in Sunnyvale. Atari opened the first Pizza Time in an abandoned supermarket in San Jose in 1977. Nolan didn't want to stop there. He envisioned a chain of Pizza Times with franchises all over the world. Manny Gerard thought one Pizza Time was one too many and wanted to sell it. Before leaving Atari, Nolan bought back his idea from Warner for half a million dollars.

Unlike McDonald's, where you grab a burger and run, Pizza Time is a hangout, like Al's on *Happy Days*. It's a nickel-and-dime business. The idea is to get the maximum number of nickels. Instead of jukeboxes, Pizza Time has video games. The switch is that the prime income is coming from the games, and the pizza is just something to keep people playing them. The jukebox at Al's was to keep them ordering burgers and shakes. The entertainment provided by the robots is free. Robots are cheaper than real entertainers. The robots aren't even that sophisticated. Nolan wasn't using advanced robot technology at Pizza Time. It was mechanical technology. However, when he went out to sell Pizza Time Theater, Nolan stood for advanced-technology entertainment, and Pizza Time appeared to be advanced-technology entertainment.

While Nolan was opening his second pizza parlor, in Sunnyvale, Robert Brock, the largest domestic Holiday Inn franchisee in America, was at his Topeka headquarters figuring out his next move. An ex-Holiday Inn executive working at Pizza Time Theater recommended that he become a Pizza Time franchisee. Impressed with the financial report for the two Theaters in operation, Brock agreed, in exchange for getting the franchise at cut-rate, to co-develop 200 restaurants in sixteen midwestern and southern states where he already had twenty-five Holiday Inns.

A few months before Brock was to open his first PTT franchise in January 1980, two of his executives discovered at an amusement park trade show a young inventor named Aaron Fletcher of Orlando, Florida, whose performing robots, they were convinced, were better than Nolan's. Fletcher told them he was the best animator in the country and the best three-dimensional animator in the world. When Brock heard this he grabbed the next plane to Orlando. Nolan had told him that he and Disney were the only ones with robot animals, and here was this guy who owned a company called Creative Engineering, Inc., employing twenty-five people and turning out about a million dollars' worth of robots a year.

Two weeks after returning to Topeka, Brock no longer

wanted to be a franchisee; he wanted to be a franchiser. Brock demanded that Nolan tear up the contract. Nolan refused. Brock went ahead anyway and negotiated a contract with Fletcher. Nolan sued Brock for breach of contract, and Brock countersued Nolan for misrepresentation. Creative Engineering produced a bear named Billy Bob Broccoli and seven other characters plus skits in return for 20 percent of Brock's new company, ShowBiz Pizza.

It cost approximately $1.25 million to build a ShowBiz Pizza unit, including eight robots, scenery, fifty video games, and pizza ovens. Pizza Time Theater, which was a little larger, cost $1.6 million for the package. The pizza pie cost $10.15. The average customer, a family of four, spent between $22 and $24 in ninety minutes, which is more than they spent at any other self-service fast food restaurant, including Pizza Hut, the largest national pizza chain.

By the end of 1982 there were 200 Pizza Times and 75 ShowBiz's. Both chains expected 1,000 units worldwide by 1985. According to their settlement, Brock will be giving Nolan a percentage of ShowBiz's annual gross revenues from the first 160 restaurants over the next fourteen years, a figure Nolan sees reaching $50 million, assuming ShowBiz and Pizza Time are still in business.

* * *

Nolan's first start-up after selling Atari to Warner was a computer-peripheral company called Axlon that he and John Vurich, inventor of the computerized pinball machine, started in Sunnyvale in March 1980. Today, Axlon is just one of the dozen garage shops doing business as part of Catalyst Technologies, a high-tech commune of highly speculative ventures Nolan set up in December 1981.

Catalyst is the Caldor of technology. In one part of the building, a team of engineers make robots; in another a high-resolution TV is being developed. Headquarters of a computer camp is across the hall. In the back, a group of engineers is moving out while another group is moving in. When a Catalyst company grows to the point where it has its team and product together, it moves out and a new start-up moves in.

Nolan never intended to sell pizza for the rest his life. He would rather focus a small team of talent on a product concept that is slightly ahead of its time. Nolan is doing what film studios like Warner Brothers did in the thirties, forties, and fifties, signing up as many actors and actresses as they could, hoping ten would become big stars. Nolan looks over the field and tries to spot holes in the market where he can fit a proven technology he's packaged in high quantities, the way a quarterback looks for holes in the opposition's defense. Then he and about fifty other companies with identical products run like mad to market.

When Nolan started Atari in the early seventies, most of the technology being used was pre–Second World War. Now there seems to be a surge of postwar technology for aggressive, gutsy entrepreneurs like Nolan to tap into. The advantage of start-ups such as Catalyst is their small size; they are able to move more quickly on a product concept than a big company and can take risks a big company won't take. If Nolan wanted to create a new product at Atari, he would first have to convince Manny Gerard at Warner. Now he's rich enough to bankroll any product he wants and charismatic enough to attract the best talent to develop it.

In the first year that Catalyst was in business, Nolan was flooded by young would-be entrepreneurs with no business expertise who wanted to come under his (Catalyst's) umbrella. The phenomenon is similar to that of students applying to school. In Catalyst's case, one out of 110 applicants has been accepted. Nolan's looking for innovative ideas and uses of technology. That eliminates quite a number of applicants.

The entrepreneurs who are accepted have ideas similar to those Nolan developed on his own. To avoid the usual start-up mistakes, Catalyst provides them with office space, telephones, copy machine, water coolers, a trained staff, and all the administrative details that can boggle a creative force, in return for a piece of the action. Essentially, Nolan puts the key in the door; all the entrepreneur needs to do is roll up his sleeves and go to work.

Nolan thinks the next hot technology after home computers will be personal robots. He put out over a million bucks to seed Androbots, which made BOB (Brains on Board), a three-foot-high robot with flashing red eyes. The eyes are really ultrasonic and heat-sensitive infrared sensors, which enable BOB to roam around the room without knocking into the furniture. BOB doesn't walk the dog or empty the trash. His brother will, but he hasn't arrived yet. It will be at least another year before he's ready.

Had a company announced that it is working on a

typewriter that has a built-in microphone and will print everything you tell it to and then the company puts out what it has developed so far—a typewriter that understands one word—that typewriter would be the equivalent of BOB. There are enough people willing to put down $2,500 to $3,000 to have BOB as a novelty. BOB is a hype for something to come that will pay for itself. A person buys BOB because he's cute and because he knows BOB is the first step toward a robot that will walk the dog and throw out the trash. A robot like that costs about $5 million, which is a lot of money for walking a dog. A dog would drag BOB down the street and through the park if BOB tried to walk it. BOB can't get over a door ledge. A person buying BOB will have to build a house just so BOB can get around. BOB has a hard time with steps. He needs ramps or elevators to get from floor to floor. If a person wants BOB to fetch a beer, he will need a special electronic refrigerator, but for $2,500, what does he expect?

Heathkit had a robot called HAL that did about as much as BOB and cost only $1,200, but nobody talked about HAL. The difference between Androbot and Heathkit is Nolan, whom the media loves to talk about.

* * *

"Give me your best table," Nolan demanded, slipping the head waiter a wad of money with Chuck E. Cheese's picture on it.

"Right this way, sir," responded the waiter and showed Nolan and his guest, an analyst from a major Wall Street brokerage, to the best table in the Lion and Compass, a restaurant Nolan built because there wasn't a decent place in which to eat in Sunnyvale. There was a white Princess telephone by the table and a stock market ticker at the bar. Nolan was wearing a brown suit with rather wide lapels, a blue shirt, and a brown tie with yellow flecks that looked like asteroids.

His expertise is not in electronics or in programming. His talent is his extraordinary ability to sell technology, generally on a one-to-one basis. This is how he earns a living, which is estimated to be more than seventy million dollars, including Pizza Time Theaters and its 225 locations, Catalyst Technologies, a restaurant, a condo in Aspen, a townhouse in Georgetown, a Parisian palace with the Eiffel Tower in the backyard, a Folger mansion up in Woodside, and a $3,800,000 Learjet that Gerald Ford, Francis Ford Coppola, and Vice President George Bush have flown in.

Nolan is a goodwill ambassador, the Colonel Sanders of electronics. He doesn't do much engineering. He still has an oscilloscope in his house, but if he had the time, he'd rather spend it skiing. He spends most mornings at Pizza Time and afternoons at Catalyst, when he's not opening another Pizza Time or checking out some new technology. Along the way he's met some pretty extraordinary people he never would have met if he weren't a bit extraordinary himself. To them, he's known as the "video game guy." To the old gang, he's still "King Pong." If a movie were made of his life, Nolan says, he would like Gene Wilder to play him, but he means Robert Redford.

Nolan's relationship to the analyst is like Ray Kassar's.

The Rise and Fall of Atari

Over lunch Nolan told the analyst how great he was. A few weeks later a copy of the analyst's report, praising Nolan, appeared on Nolan's desk. Nolan began thinking that if this analyst reported he was great then he must be even greater than he thought, and he told the next analyst he had lunch with that he was even greater.

Another report appeared on Nolan's desk. Then another analyst showed up for lunch and the progression continued this way. It was like the demonstration schools use to show how nuclear fission works: Mousetraps with Ping-Pong balls on them are set up in a box, someone throws a Ping-Pong ball into the box, and it triggers off a couple more balls, which trigger off a couple more, and before long balls are flying all over the place. As Nolan's reputation becomes greater and greater, more people want to buy Pizza Time franchises, more budding entrepreneurs knock on Catalyst's door, more investors beg Nolan to take their money.

When Nolan sold Atari he signed an agreement that he would not compete with Atari for seven years. In early 1983 Nolan was bragging to the press that on October 1, 1983, at 10 A.M., when the agreement expired, he would be out on the street with a new generation of arcade games that would push the video game medium to a new level, from shoot-em-up games to more educational ones. These "revolutionary" games were built on a new technology developed by Delman, Hector, and Rotberg. Nolan fully expected that his new video game company, Sente, a subsidiary of Pizza Time Theater, whose 225 locations with 75–100 games in each make them the largest user in the country, to control 40 percent of an anticipated $900 million market.

On April 7 Atari filed suit to enjoin Nolan from elaborating any further until the noncompete contract expired. In May Atari dropped the suit when Nolan signed an agreement to sell Atari the rights to the home video version of his new games. Nolan had no intention of marketing the home version of his video games himself; Atari, desperate for product, was eager to sign up Nolan in their quest for new talent that so far included the rights to video games created by LucasFilms, home-video rights to Williams Electronics arcade games, and video rights to MCA Studios' films.

By buying the rights to Nolan's Sente games, Atari was not necessarily buying the technology that implements these games. Nolan could possibly come out with a laser-type arcade game with Smellorama, which is played upside down while floating around in a booth, that Atari might not be able to exploit with their current home video game technology. In that case, Atari's advantage in making a deal with Nolan was to prevent Nolan from making a deal with one of Atari's rivals, who might develop a home video system that could exploit Nolan's games. Nolan had set out to do battle with Atari, but instead they ended up in bed together.

*   *   *

On July 7, 1983, Warner announced that Ray Kassar had resigned as chairman and chief executive of Atari. He was replaced on September 6 by James J. Morgan, the forty-one-year-old executive vice president of marketing for the American cigarette operations of Philip Morris, Inc. Morgan owns a home video game but has no knowledge of computers. The analyst was amazed that Kassar lasted as long as he did. He was not amazed that Warner replaced him with another top executive with marketing skills and no technical ability. The announcement had no apparent effect on the Warner stock price. Although a Warner spokesman denied that Kassar had been ousted, the analyst thought it was suspicious that Warner was able to find a replacement immediately.

About ten days before his appointment was announced, Morgan had lunch with Steve Ross. The next day he had lunch with other Warner executives, and the day after that he received the offer. The whole thing happened in three days. It was believed Morgan's salary will exceed ten million dollars over the next seven years.

On visiting Atari for the first time, Morgan couldn't believe Atari was spread among so many buildings. Only two of nine executives who would be reporting to him had offices in the same building. Morgan said he would meet with his top executives for two hours every morning, just so the executives could talk to one another, which apparently they had not been doing under Kassar. Steve Ross, in turn, promised that he would speak to Morgan daily. Despite the dip video games have taken, Morgan predicted that cartridge sales would increase by 35% in 1983 to 100 million units, and to 155 million the following year. He expected home computer sales to triple to 4.9 million units

ZAP!

in 1983 and to 7.5 in 1984. Selling computers, it would seem, will not be much different from selling cigarettes. The analyst, however, didn't believe a cigarette salesman was the solution to Atari's problem. "It's astonishing to see how much a huge conglomerate like Warner could be so dependent upon one division."

Epilogue
Fall 1983

FROM a departing plane, Silicon Valley looks less like a microchip and more like a giant K-Mart, with the different aisles, the bargain chips here, the meat and potato chips there, and the liquor section down there. You can go to a small boutique and most likely find what you want, and yet you can go to a K-Mart, which is a hundred times bigger, and you may never find what you want. Silicon Valley is no longer the place for development and technology that it was. Now it's a meat market. What is happening to the Valley happened to Detroit, except there it was spread out over forty years. There are more companies in the Valley now than before, but it's not the hot spot it was. More companies are thinking about moving to the Midwest, since "cheap" labor down South is no longer cheap. Much of Silicon Valley will probably end up in Detroit, where all those auto workers are standing around with nothing to do.

ZAP!

Atari occupies less of the Valley than it did a year ago, particularly since it laid off 3,000 workers and moved video game and computer manufacturing offshore. From the air, these empty facilities look like sockets with missing chips. In one year the price of the Atari 800 computer fell from $800 to $165. The UCS 2600, which cost $150 at best, now sells for under $40. There have been many internal shake-ups at corporate headquarters over the past year, and the merging of the video games and computer divisions will probably mean more empty sockets.

It's an entirely new screen at Atari. A new telecommunications division, Ataritel, whose first product was expected to be a telephone with computer capabilities that could control home appliances, was added. Some things haven't changed. Peter Wensberg was replaced as president of the division only nine months after coming to Atari from Polaroid, where he was a marketing executive. Ataritel now seems to be a dead issue.

An original Computer Space still stands outside Steve Bristow's office. Bristow is the only one of Nolan's Seven Princes left at Atari. Bill White, the old Atari minister of finance, left the company when Warner arrived. Gil Williams, who was in charge of manufacturing, left in 1981, around the time Delman, Hector, and Rotberg formed Videa. Joe Keenan, former president of Kee Games and Atari, until recently had been president of Pizza Time Theater.

As the plane heads over the Pizza Time Theater in downtown Sunnyvale, a garbage truck is hauling away a load of pizza crust and paper cups, while another truck

160

loaded with quarters drives off in another direction. The No Smoking sign goes off as Steve Jobs, the young chairman of Apple, can be seen zooming home on his motorcycle. Over there, Steve Wozniak, who had gone back to school to get his degree and is back with Apple, is shooting a Datsun commercial. A stewardess hands out an in-flight magazine with Nolan's picture on the cover as the plane banks over ByVideo, a shop-at-home Catalyst company run by Gene Lipkin. Videa was bought by Nolan for $2.2 million; the Three Stooges, now part of Sente, are in another building, while a new start-up moved into their old space at Catalyst. To the east is Nolan's restaurant, Lion and Compass, and there's Nolan zipping by in his Lear jet. October 1, 1983, the expiration date of Nolan's agreement not to compete with Atari, has come around. A new generation of video games, based on laser-disk technology, are being shipped to arcades around the country: unfortunately, none are Nolan's. Due to production problems, Sente's debut will have to wait a few months.

Al Alcorn, the engineer who built Pong, is taking it easy up at his trout farm in the mountains near Carmel. Al dropped out around Missile Command and is part of the "beach club," a select group of ex-Atarians being paid to do nothing. Then the plane ascends into the haze, and the last thing that can be seen in the gathering darkness is a solitary light coming from a garage window off in a corner of the Valley, where somebody is working on something.

*Primary Sources**

Ira Bettelman, C. A. Robinson Co., distributors
Stephen Bristow, Atari vice president, engineering
Nolan Bushnell, inventor of the video game
Suzie Crocker, Pizza Time Theater corporate communications
   manager
Howard Delman, engineer/game designer
Bruce Entin, Atari spokesman
Roger Hector, game designer
Don Hoefler, *Microelectronics News* newsletter editor
Harry Jenkins, Atari design research, corporate division
Ginny Juhnke, Atari public relations
Midway public relations spokesperson
Carl Nielsen, Atari director, LSI design and test

*Note the above positions are of summer, 1982.

The Rise and Fall of Atari

Donald Osborne, Atari vice president, sales and marketing
Lyle Rains, Atari director
Gilbert Rosborne, historian
Ed Rotberg, game designer
Howard Winters, local historian
Steve Wright, Atari director, special programs

Bibliography

Berg, Eric: "A.T.&T. and Coleco in Video Game Venture," *New York Times*, September 1983, pp. D1, D5.

Bernstein, Peter W.: "Atari and the Video-Game Explosion," *Fortune*, July 27, 1981, pp. 40–46.

Bloom, Steve: "From Cutoffs to Pinstripes," *Video Games*, December 1982, pp. 37–50, 80.

Bloom, Steve: *Video Invaders*, Arco, 1982.

Boraiko, Allen A.: "The Chip," *National Geographic*, October 1982, pp. 421–456.

Bowles, Jerry: "Cashing In on the Micro Chips," *Village Voice*, March 30, 1982, pp. 67–69.

Brown, Andrew C.: "Cashing In on the Cartridge Trade," *Fortune*, November 15, 1982, pp. 125–6ff.

Business Week: "Atari's Struggle to Stay Ahead," p. 56.

The Rise and Fall of Atari

Business Week: "Nolan Bushnell's Newest Brainstorms," February 28, 1983, p. 54.

———: "The New Entrepreneurs," April 18, 1983, pp. 79–82.

———: "Big Business Tries to Imitate the Entrepreneurial Spirit," April 18, 1983, pp. 84–87.

Covert, Colin: "Video Gamesmanship," *Ambassador*, August 1982, pp. 29–37.

Dolan, Carrie: "Land of Plenty," *Wall Street Journal*, August 2, 1983, pp. 1, 14.

Financial World: "Coleco's Comeback," August 15, 1982, pp. 25–26.

Goldfein, Donna: "Raymond E. Kassar of Atari, Inc.," *Skylite*, January/February 1983, pp. 21–23.

Johnston, Moira: "Silicon Valley," *National Geographic*, October 1982, pp. 421–456.

Kanner, Bernice: "Can Atari Stay Ahead of the Game?" *New York*, August 16, 1982, pp. 15–17.

Kilday, Gregg: "Amazing Atari!," *Home Video*, March 1983, pp. 27–31.

Kinkead, Gwen: "High Profits from a Weird Pizza Combination," *Fortune*, July 26, 1982, pp. 62–66.

Kirby, Christopher D.: *The Video Game Industry*, Sanford C. Bernstein & Co., December 1982.

Landro, Laura: "Warner's Atari Staff Facing Shake-Up; Merger of Video, Computer Divisions Set," *Wall Street Journal*, May 31, 1983.

ZAP!

Lewin, Tamar: "A Myriad of Problems for Warner," *New York Times*, December 19, 1982, p. F8.

Lueck, Thomas J.: "Warner Cuts Corporate Staff by 250," *New York Times*, October 14, 1983, pp. D1, D6.

Mamis, Robert A.: "The Pied Piper of Sunnyvale, Inc.," March 1983, pp. 57–66.

Marbacj, William D., with Pamela Abramson: "From Atari to Androbot," *Newsweek*, November 15, 1982, p. 123.

New York Post: "Atari, Coleco Launch $850M Legal Battle," December 9, 1982, p.68.

————: "Move Over, R2D2," June 9, 1983, p. 13.

————: "Atari Removes a Key Executive," December 9, 1982.

————:"Atari Replaces Hed of Unit after 9 Months," September 1983.

————: "Playing Video Games for Fun and Profit," March 29, 1982, p. D4.

Noble, Kenneth B.: "Two Charged in Atari Stock Sale, *New York Times*, September 27, 1983, pp. D1, D8.

Nulty, Peter: "Why the Craze Won't Quit," *Fortune*, November 15, 1982, pp. 114–124.

Owen, David: "Invasion of the Asteroids," *Esquire*, February 1981, pp. 58–62.

————: "The Second Coming of Nolan Bushnell, *Playboy*, June 1983, pp. 127, 134, 248–257.

Pillsbury, Anne B.: "Warner's Fall From Grace," *Fortune*, January 10, 1983, pp. 82–83.

The Rise and Fall of Atari

Pollack, Andrew: "Chief Is Replaced at Troubled Atari," *New York Times*, July 8, 1983, pp. D1–D2.

————: "The Game Turns Serious at Atari," *New York Times*, December 19, 1982.

San Francisco Chronicle: "We Slip into Nerdism, but We're Regular Guys," June 2, 1982, p. 37.

Sansweet, Stephen J.: "Designers Are Stars in Video-Game Field; Some Get Fan Mail," *Wall Street Journal,* January 19, 1983, pp. 1, 22.

Schwartz, Tony: "Steve Ross: On the Spot," *New York*, January 24, 1983.

Shannon, Dan: "Games Are Hard Work," *Village Voice*, March 30, 1982, pp. 80–81.

Skow, John: "Games That Play People," *Time*, January 18, 1982, pp. 50–58.

Smilon, Marvin: "Warner Boss Target in Westchester Theater Probe," *New York Post*, December 14, 1982, p. 13.

Time: "The Seeds of Success," February 15, 1982, pp. 40–41.

————: "Zapped," June 13, 1983, p. 50.

USA Today: "Atari, Bushnell Agree," May 27, 1983.

————: "Times Demand High-Tech Stocks," June 20, 1983, p. 6B.

Trachtman, Paul: "A Generation Meets Computers and They Are Friendly," *Smithsonian*, September 1981, pp. 50–61.

Wayne, Leslie: "Atari Moving Most Production," *New York Times*, February 23, 1983, p. D5.

Wieder, Robert: "A Fistful of Quarters," *Oui*, September, 1974, pp. 59–62, 124–128.

————: "The Return of King Pong," *Success*, February 1983, pp. 17–19.

Index

Activision, 94–96, 110, 117, 140
Adding machines, 9
Advanced Microdevices, 13, 93
Adversary, 63
Akerman, Nick, 130
Alcorn, Al, 25–30, 36, 44–45, 46, 57, 69–70, 74–76, 82, 161
Allied Leisure, 39, 63
American Express, 129
Ampex Corporations, 16, 21, 22, 23, 25
Analogue computers, 26
Androbots, 152
Andy Capp's, Pong installed at, 28–30
Anglin, Noah, 70
Anti-Aircraft, 47
Apple, 56–57, 110, 160, 161
Apple I, 56
Apple II, 139

Arcade video games:
   home video vs., 85–86, 90
   initial skepticism toward, 22
   licensing of, for home video, 79–80, 111, 117–118
Aries, 8
Army, U.S., video training used by, 99
Asteroids, 17, 80, 81, 84–86, 89, 96, 111
A.T.&T. (American Telephone and Telegraph), 145
Atari:
   competition and, 39–40, 63
   early home video of, 45–49
   home computers of, 95, 138
   incorporation of, 23–24
   inventory bind of, 62, 64, 131
   LucasFilm and, 134, 144, 156
   marketing of, 64–68

Index

Atari (*cont.*):
  mismanagement of, 124–132
  naming of, 23–24
  old vs. new management of, 73
  pinball and, 66, 83–84
  production line of, 34
  reorganization of, 69–70, 71–73, 127–128
  security at, 71–72
  Space Invaders licensed by, 79–80
  typical programmers at, 87–88, 90–92
  VCS of, 53–54, 56, 94, 96
  (*See also* Warner Communications)
Atari 400 computer, 95, 138–139
Atari 800 computer, 95
Atari 5200 Super VCS, 104, 119, 139
Atari Baseball, 99
Atari Japan, 41
Atarian, 84
Ataritel, 160
Avalanche, 78
Axlon, 150–151
AY38500 chips, 51–52, 63

Babbage, Charles, 9
Baer, Ralph, 18–20, 46
Bailey, Donna, 88
Bally's Midway, 76, 142
  as Atari rival, 39, 47, 53, 80
  Pong and, 31–32
Basketball, 95
Battlezone, 96, 99

Beckman, Arnold, 13, 14
Beckman Instruments, 13
Bell Laboratories, 12, 145
Benchley Park, London, computer production at, 10
Berkeley, University of California at, 25, 81, 94
Berserk, 89, 90, 117
Bettelman, Ira, 32, 37, 39–40
Billboard, video game chart of, 117
Billy Bob Broccoli, 150
"Blue boxes," 55
BOB (Brains on Board), 152–153
Bocciball, 79–80
Breakout, 53, 54–55, 78
Bristow, Steve, 21–24, 35, 37, 39, 45, 81, 103–104, 160
Brock, Robert, 149–150
Brown, Bob, 48–49, 69
Bryan, Larry, 23
Burroughs, 11
Bushnell, Nolan, 14, 20, 25–26
  as Atari executive, 41–43, 52–61
  Atari founding and, 23–24
  background of, 15–16
  Computer Space built by, 17–18, 22
  after leaving Atari, 147–156, 161
  at Nutting Associates, 21–22
  Warner Communications and, 57–61, 64–68
ByVideo, 161

Index

Calculators, 9
Canyon Bomber, 82, 97
Cartridges:
  categories of, 90
  compatibility of, 118–119
  future sales of, 157
  replaceable, 52
Catalyst Technologies, 151–152,
  154–155, 160
Centipede, 88
Channel F, 52
Chips:
  AY38500, 51–52, 63
  manufacture of, 20
  microprocessor, 53–54
  random-access memory, 52
Cinematronics, 75
Circuits (see Integrated circuits)
Clevite, 13
Code, computer deciphering of,
  9–10
Coleco, 52, 63, 116–118, 133,
  145
ColecoVision, 116–118, 133, 139
Color, video games in, 21, 52
Commodore VIC-20 computer,
  138–139
Computer Age, early days of, 8–
  11
Computer Space, 160
  development of, 17–18, 22
  marketing of, 22–23
  two-man version of, 25
Computers:
  analogue, 26
  digital, 8–9, 26

fixed-purpose game-playing
  machines vs., 18
military applications of, 9–11
personal, 55–57, 137–139
Spacewar played on, 16
telephones and, 160
Control Data, 3, 82
Cosmos, 82
CPU (central processing unit),
  11
Crane, David, 93, 94–95
Crawford, Gordon, 59
Creative Engineering, Inc., 149
Crossman, W. E., 8
Cyan Engineering, 53

Dabney, Ted, 22, 23, 24
"Darlene," 45
Decure, Joe, 54
Defender, 89, 90
Delman, Howard, 71, 73–75, 82,
  96–99
  on Asteroids design team, 82,
  96
  background of, 73
  Videa and, 101–102, 160
Demon Attack, 96
Dig Dug, 89
Digital computers, 9–10, 26
Digital Equipment Corp., 18
Dirtbike, 82
Disney:
  Atari merger declined by, 149
  robots of, 149
Dodgem, 42
Donkey Kong, 88–89, 117–118

Index

Dukes of Hazzard toy products, 129
Dungeons and Dragons, 88

Edmunds, Larry, 53
Elimination, 36
Emmett, Jay, 129
Enders, Bill, 19
ENIAC computer, 11, 54
Enigma machine, 9–10
E.T., 112, 117, 120, 132
Evans and Southerland, 144

Fairchild Camera and Instrument, 13–14, 52, 93
    as Atari rival, 63
Fairchild F8 microprocessor, 52
Fairfield Semiconductor, 14
Fidelity Venture Associates, 50
Fire Truck, 97
First Dimension, 52
Fletcher, Aaron, 149–150
Football, 82, 84
Fortune, 39
Freeway, 94, 117
Frenzy, 42
Frisbee, 144
Frogger, 117–118
Fulop, Rob, 96

Galaxy Game:
    invention of, 18
    marketing of, 23
Game cartridges (*see* Cartridges)
General Electric, 19
General Instrument, 51, 63

Gerard, Emanuel, 59–60, 62–68, 110, 112–116, 148
Go, 24
Gold Rush, 2, 6
Gotcha, 39
Grantrak, 42
Graphics:
    color, 21, 52
    holographic, 67, 74, 76, 82, 87
    line- vs. grid-drawing in, 75
    raster-scan generation of, 28
    realism of, 20–21, 142
    video disks and, 142
Grass Valley, 53, 148
Gravitar, 89
Grubb, William F. X., 96
Gun Fight, 47

HAL, 153
Hangman, 95
Harrison, Bill, 19
Hasbro Industries, 123, 129
Hauer, Gustave, 129
Headhunters, 2
Heathkit, 153
Hector, Roger, 98–102, 107, 160
Hendy Ironworks, 8–9
Hercules, 84
Hewlett, Bill, 1, 13, 55
Hewlett-Packard, 1, 13, 55, 74
Hockey, 94
Hoff, Ted, 134–135
Holmes, Geoff, 110–111
Holography, 67, 74, 76, 82, 89
Holosonics, 101

Index

Home information services, 145–
146
Home Pong, 45–49, 57
Home video games, 45–49
  arcade video games vs., 85–
    86, 90
  in color, 52
  craze in, 78
  marketing problems of, 63–
    70
  personal computers and, 138–
    140
  programmable, 52–53
  replaceable cartridges for, 52
  standardization of, 118–119
  stereo systems used with, 49
  televisions and, 17, 19, 27–28,
    46–47
  (See also Video games)
Horwitz, Leonard, 129–130
Hula Hoop, marketing of, 37–39,
  40, 143

IBM, 11, 70
  Intel and, 135–137
Imagic, 96, 110, 117, 140
Integrated circuits:
  invention and development of,
    20
  large-scale, 46–47
  as microprocessors, 53–54
  very large-scale, 92–93
  (See also Chips)
Intel, 3, 56
  Fairchild origins of, 13, 93
  IBM and, 135–137

microprocessor development
  by, 54
Intellivision, 96, 116, 133, 139
ITT (International Telephone and
  Telegraph), 13

Jaws, 47
Jenkins, Harry, 71, 74–76, 82,
  104–107
Jet Fighter, 82
Jobs, Steve, 54–57, 160
Jubilee, 8

Kaboom, 94
Kangaroo, 89
Kaplan, Larry, 93
Kassar, Ray, 64–65, 67, 78–79,
  83, 108–111, 154
  Atari reorganization and, 69–
    70, 71–72, 127
  insider trading charges against,
    125–126
Kay, Alan, 105, 134
Kee games, 36, 45
Keenan, Joe, 36, 44–45, 57, 64,
  67, 160
Knitting machines, computers
  and, 9

Large-scale integrated (LSI) cir-
  cuits, 46–47
Leavy, Jim, 94
Lee, Harold, 54
Libby's, 8
Lipkin, Gene, 44, 57, 70, 161
Lloyd's Electronics, 52

Index

Lockheed, 8
Logg, Ed, 82
LucasFilm, Atari and, 134, 144, 156
Lunar Lander, 75, 89, 96

Magnavox, 19
  Odyssey game systems of, 46, 47, 63
Markkula, Armas "Mike," 56–57
Masks (screens), refinement of, 20
Mattel, 96, 116–117, 133
Mayfield Fund, 50
MCA Studios, 57, 134, 156
Meadows Games, 47
Melin, Arthur "Spud," 37–38
Meyer, Steve, 53–54
Microchips (see Chips)
Microprocessors, 53–54
Middle Earth, 84
Midway (see Bally's Midway)
Miller, Alan, 93, 94–95
Missile Command, 79, 161
Moffett Field, 1, 8
Morgan, James J., 156–158
Mousetrap, 117–118
Murphy, Michael, Jr., 5–7
Music, video games and, 49, 97
Muzak, 145

Namco, 111
NASA, 8, 12, 95
National Semiconductor, 3, 51
  Adversary system of, 63
  Fairchild origins of, 13, 93

Night Driver, 53
99/4A computer, 138–139
Noyce, Robert, 20
Nutting Associates, 21–22, 25, 28
Nutting, Bill, 22

Odak, Perry, 121
Odyssey, 46
  marketing of, 47
Odyssey 2, 63
Osborne, Don, 83, 85

Packard, Dave, 1
Pac-Man, 18, 88–89, 90, 111
PDP-11 computer, 18
Personal computers, 55–57, 137–140
Pin Pong, 42
Pinball games, Atari and, 66, 83–84
Pit Fall, 117
Pitts, Bill, 18, 23
Pizza Time Theater, 147–150, 154–155, 159
Plimpton, George, 133
Pong, 85
  derivatives of, 36–37, 39
  distribution of, 32–33
  First installation of, 28–30
  Midway and, 31–32
Pong Doubles, 36, 39

Quadrapong, 37, 39
Quinn, Tom, 48
Qume, 3

Index

Raiders of the Lost Ark, 112, 117, 120
Rains, Lyle, 81–82
Ramtek, 39, 47
Random-access memory (RAM) chips, 52
Raster scan, 27, 75
RCA, 19, 51, 63
  Studio 2 system of, 62
Replaceable cartridges, 42
C.A. Robinson distributors, 33
Robots, 148–150, 152–153
Rommel, Erwin, enigma machine used by, 10
Ross, Steve, 58, 60, 110, 113, 130–131
Rotberg, Ed, 98, 99–100, 160
Rusch, Bill, 19
Russell, Steve, 16

Sanders Associates, 18–19, 46
San Jose State, 4
Scientific American, 72, 108
Screens (masks), improvement of, 20
Screens, video:
  image generation on, 27
  refinement of, 20–21
Sea Wolf, 47
Sears, Roebuck, 48–49
Securities and Exchange Commission, Kasser investigated by, 126
Semiconductors, 20
Sente, 156, 161
7400 series TTL, 17

Shockley, William, 12–14
Shockley Semiconductor, 13–14
ShowBiz Pizza, 150
Silicon, semiconductor properties of, 20
Silicon Valley, 1–8
  decline of, 159–160
  drinking in, 2, 3–5
  housing in, 4–5
  as world's semiconductor capital, 2
Smokey Joe, 97
Sound, Pong's use of, 28
Space Invaders, 18, 76–78, 84–86
  licensing of, for home video, 79, 111
Space Race, 36, 39
Space Wars, 75
Spacewar, 16, 17, 18
Spies, industrial, 2, 72
Spring II, 82
Sprint 2, 53
Stanford University, 1, 4, 18, 74
Steeple Chase, 82
"Stella," 54
Stereo, home video applications of, 49
Studio 2, 62
Sunnyvale, Calif., industrialization in, 7–8
Super Breakout, 82
Superbug, 97
Superman, 84
SuperPong, 39
Surround, 95

175

Index

Taito Corporation, 76–78, 111
Tandy TRS-80 computer, 138–139
Tank, 37, 47, 81, 85
Tank II, 47
Telephones:
  "blue boxes" connected to, 55
  with computer capabilities, 104, 160
Teleprompter, 19
Television:
  home video games played on, 17, 19, 27–28, 46–47
  image generation on, 27–28
Tennis, 94
Texas Instruments, 17, 138
Texas Instruments 99/4A computer, 138–139
Time Inc., 50
Touch-Me, 42
Transistor-transistor logic (TTL), 17, 26, 52
Transistors:
  invention and development of, 13–14, 145
  on microchips, 20
  vacuum tubes vs., 12
TRS-80 computer, 138

Universal Studios, 57
Utah, University of, 16

Vacuum tubes, computers built with, 10, 11, 12
Valentine, Don, 49–50, 56

VCS (see Video computer system)
Vector-generated hardware, 75
Venture Capital Management Services, 49
Very large-scale integrated (VLSI) circuits, 92–93
VIC-20 computer, 138–139
Videa, 101–102, 160, 161
Video computer system (VCS), 53–54, 56, 94
Video disks, 142
Video games:
  in color, 21, 52
  computers vs. fixed-purpose game-playing machines for, 17–18
  designing of, 88–92
  future of, 144–146
  military applications of, 18–19, 99–100
  as new form of entertainment, 77–78
  sound generation in, 28
  telephone wiretransmission of, 145
  (See also Arcade video games; Home video games)
Video Music, 49
Video Pinball, 82
Vurich, John, 150

WALL Street Journal, 41
Warner-Amex Cable Communications, 129

Index

Warner Bros.-Seven Arts, 59
Warner Communications, 62–70
  Atari acquired by, 57–61, 62,
    110
  class-action suits against, 128–
    129
  financial analysis of, 65–66,
    109–111, 112–115, 119–
    120, 123–124, 128–129,
    133–135
  insider trader scandal and,
    125–126
  Knickerbocker Toy division of,
    123–124, 129
Weiss, Solomon, 129–130
Wensberg, Peter, 160
Westinghouse, 8

Wham-O, 37–38, 40, 144
White, Bill, 160
Whitehead, Bob, 93
Williams, Gil, 160
Williams Electronics, 156
Wind Tunnel, 8
Winters, Howard, 6
World War II, computers in,
    10–11
Wozniak, Steve, 55–57, 160–
    161

Xicor, 3
X-Y monitors, 53

Zenith, 19
Zylog, 3